Studies in Caribbean Languages

Chief Editor: John R. Rickford

Managing Editor: Joseph T. Farquharson

In this series:

1. Irvine-Sobers, G. Alison. The acrolect in Jamaica: The architecture of phonological variation.

2. Forbes-Barnett, Marsha. Dual aspectual forms and event structure in Caribbean English Creoles.

3. Sherriah, André Ché. A tale of two dialect regions: Sranan's 17th-century English input.

ISSN: 2627-1893

A tale of two dialect regions

Sranan's 17th-century English input

André Ché Sherriah

language
science
press

André Ché Sherriah. 2019. *A tale of two dialect regions: Sranan's 17th-century English input* (Studies in Caribbean Languages 3). Berlin: Language Science Press.

ISSN: 2627-1893
DOI:10.5281/zenodo.2625403
Source code available from www.github.com/langsci/179
Collaborative reading: paperhive.org/documents/remote?type=langsci&id=179

Cover and concept of design: Ulrike Harbort
Typesetting: André Ché Sherriah, Felix Kopecky, Sebastian Nordhoff
Proofreading: Alexis Michaud, Amir Ghorbanpour, Andreas Hölzl, Bev
Erasmus, Eran Asoulin, Ivica Jeđud, Jeroen van de Weijer, Marijana Janjić,
Sandra Auderset
Fonts: Linux Libertine, Libertinus Math, Arimo, DejaVu Sans Mono
Typesetting software: XƎLATEX

Language Science Press
Unter den Linden 6
10099 Berlin, Germany
langsci-press.org

Storage and cataloguing done by FU Berlin

Freie Universität Berlin

I would like to dedicate this work to my grandmother, Dulcie Mae Roper, God rest your soul. I have never forgotten you, nor will I ever. You taught me to never give up, but to always give my all, no matter the obstacles that might block my path. Thank you.

Contents

Contents

Preface

The fundamental aim of this research is two-fold. First, it represents an attempt to pinpoint the precise origin of the early English lexical and phonetic (lexico-phonetic) influences in Sranan; i.e. whether this influence was from a single dialect, as expressed by a mono-dialectal account of origin, or from a composite of dialects from all over England, as expressed by a pan-dialectal account. Second, it introduces a new methodological tool (comprising of a statistics component, an English dialect geography component and a 17th century English migration history component) with which such linguistic reconstructive work can be done. This tool was used to ascertain the potential dialectal origins of forty-five Sranan words of English origin, alongside the dialectal origin(s) of their speakers. This was done via corroboration of the results of the independent analyses done across the three components of the tripartite methodological tool. The work relies heavily on secondary data sources for both the Sranan data and English dialectal data. The reason for this is the need to use the oldest possible lexical and phonetic information for both language varieties since the early 17th century English influence in Suriname, the country in which Sranan is spoken, ended after 1667.

Acknowledgments

This dissertation would not have been possible without the guidance and assistance of several people who in one way or another contributed and extended their valuable time and expertise in the groundwork and accomplishment of this study.

My utmost appreciation to Professor Hubert Devonish, without whose excellent supervision, this would not have been possible. Professor Devonish has challenged my abilities at all levels, thereby allowing me to surpass thresholds that I never thought it possible to surpass.

I am deeply grateful to Professor Ewart Thomas of Stanford University, who made himself available to aid me with most, if not all, my statistical analysis related matters. I would like to express my gratitude for his expertise and the patience he showed to me, a non-statistician.

Many thanks, to Dr. Karen Carpenter for her altruistic and dependable support as the coordinator of what was a very effective writing group. Her guidance and support, especially at times when what laid ahead seemed overwhelming, will not be forgotten.

I would like to thank Lubova Dubilina, who spent countless hours with me, helping to format my work. Thank you for your assistance, patience and resolve to see me complete what I started.

Last but by no means least, my sincerest gratitude to my loving and supportive parents, Augustus Sherriah, and Verna Sherriah, my best friend and brother, Courtney Smith, my dearest friends and colleagues, Audene Henry-Harvey, Daidrah Smith, Kedisha Williams, Yanique Wallace, Tashieka Burris and the countless others who supported me in more ways than one, throughout this journey.

Abbreviations

CCAT	Concentric Circle-by-concentric circle Allocation Table
CCR	Consonant Cluster Reversal
CPPE	Caribbean Plantation Pidgin English
DF	Dental Fricative
Diph	Diphthong
EC	Existing Combinations
h	Word-initial phonemic ⟨h⟩
I.O.W	Isle of White
IPA	International Phonetic Alphabet
IVDM	Input Variants Distribution Map
IVRDM	Input Variants Route Distribution Map
LexVar	Lexical Varient
LBH	Language Bioprogram Hypothesis
LVoic	Labial Voicing
Pal	Word-initial Palatal
PC	Possible Combinations
PHP	Hypertext Pre-processor
PVR	Post-vocalic /r/
RIH	Regional Input Hypothesis
SED	Survey of English Dialects
SL	Start Lect
SSA	Saramaccan, Sranna and Aukan
WSW	West South-West

1 Introduction

1.1 An interest sparked

The summer of 2004 marked the first time I, as a then undergraduate student, had ever set foot on Surinamese soil. The purpose of the trip was to collect language data on the English-lexicon creoles spoken in the country. In analysing the data collected, I began to unearth various correspondences between the phonetic shapes of words of English origin and their reflexes across Saramaccan, Sranan, and Aukan, hereafter ssa.

In March of 2007, I, as a graduate student supervising an undergraduate field-trip, went to Suriname again. On that occasion, I was fortunate enough to be able to collect additional data from other ssa settlements not previously visited during the 2004 fieldtrip. On this occasion, the goal was to determine to what degree the phenomena noticed on the 2004 fieldtrip were similar across different groups of ssa speakers. I noticed the same phonetic correspondences as well as new ones across the various ssa reflexes and their English cognates.

One correspondence observed was the production and non-production of /r/ in post-vocalic positions. Some ssa words such as Sranan's *more* [moro], Saramaccan's *work* [woroko] and Aukan's *gutter* [gotro] suggested that the English input forms had a postvocalic /r/, hereafter pvr. However, other words such as Sranan's *four* [fɔ], Saramaccan's *finger* [fɪŋga] and Aukan's *horse* [asɪ] suggested that other English input forms lacked a post-vocalic /r/; I was fascinated and my fascination led me to ask three questions:

1. Was ssa influenced by both /r/-full and /r/-less British Isles English dialects?

2. Was ssa influenced by a single British Isles English dialect, which exhibited /r/-full and /r/-less on specific lexical items?

3. Was the combination of /r/-fullness and /r/-lessness a purely Sranan phenomenon?

I had a desire to know more; I needed to know the exact origin of the patterns of correspondence and lack of correspondence thereof, with rhotic dialects of English and SSA. I also needed to ascertain why these and other patterns presented themselves across all three creoles. This linguistic curiosity led to my perusing both historical and historical-linguistic works about SSA and Suriname; some of these included: Bridenbaugh (1968), Esposito et al. (1982), Hoefte (1998), Kambel & MacKay (1999), Rens (1953), Muysken & Smith (1986), Smith (1987) and Smith & Veenstra (2001).

The insights gained from these works did their part in fuelling my interest even further. I had been working on another research topic for my dissertation, but I dropped it. I wanted to pursue my SSA interest, specifically my interest in Suriname's lingua franca, Sranan, which was the main SSA creole that I was researching during the two above-mentioned fieldtrips. With my change in interest from my previous topic and after spending years scrutinizing Sranan data, English dialectal geography data in the form of The Survey of English Dialects (Orton et al. 1962–71), and 17th century historical data from England, I broadened the focus of the research and this led to the following research questions:

1. What do lexico-phonetic correspondences between Sranan words and their English dialectal etyma tell us about where within England this influence might have originated?

2. What can one (1.) above tell us about the competing hypotheses concerning the source of lexico-phonetic input in Sranan, i.e. a pan-dialectal account versus a mono-dialectal account?

3. What kind of corroboration for or challenge to the proposed dialect area(s) do we find in the historical records?

The data and method used to address these research questions are outlined in more detail in Chapter 3. The remainder of this chapter is a presentation of a brief history of Suriname and the SSA creoles, specifically Sranan; the major problem that the research addresses, the significance of the research and an outline of the contents of the remaining chapters.

1.2 Brief history of Suriname and Sranan

1.2.1 The seventeenth century settlers

The English arrived in the West Indies in 1624, settling first in St. Christopher, present day St. Kitts. They subsequently settled Barbados in 1627 (Dunn 1973:

18), Nevis in 1628 (Wroughton 2006: 297), and Antigua and Montserrat in 1632, respectively (Forsyth 1869: 27). Of these settlements Barbados, by the 1650s, had the largest population. Its importance among the English colonies grew steadily and Barbados soon took over the function of a way station from St. Kitts, but on a far greater scale (Davies 1974). Between 1650 and 1680, for example, Barbados, with its "... swiftly acquired white population, [which was] made increasingly redundant ... after 1640 by the introduction of slave labor ... may have supplied to buccaneering, to expeditionary forces out of England, and to colonies as many as 20,000 ... [or possibly] ... 30,000 ..." people (Davies 1974: 137). Suriname was one of the colonies settled from Barbados.

British colonists, sanctioned by Lord Francis Willoughby, governor of Barbados, settled Suriname from Barbados in the early 1650s (Ehrlich 2009; Arbell 2002; Hymason 1908), after two failed attempts to do so in 1630 and 1649 (Arbell 2002: 82). Three hundred Barbadians under the command of soon to be governor, Anthony Rowse, "landed on the Surinam and Commewine rivers?" and, after making peace with the native Amerindians, gave the English a stable footing in the mainland territory (Salomon & Schwartz 1999: 414). Suriname would soon become a thriving colony due to continual migration from Barbados. By 1663, for example, the Suriname colony "... boasted a population of 1,000 Whites, 2,000 enslaved Africans and 1,000 natives scattered among fifty large and several smaller plantations" (Marley 2005: 808).

In 1664, when the French captured nearby Cayenne from the Dutch, the Portuguese Jews and their enslaved Africans who resided there were forced to move into Suriname (Redfield 2000; Friedman 1999). Willoughby granted them permission to settle in Suriname, since their affluence and planting expertise rendered them an asset to the colony (Ehrlich 2009). Consequently, by 1667, of the one hundred and eighty plantations in Suriname, six or seven of them belonged to these Portuguese Jews (Arbell 2002; Rens 1953). These Jewish plantations, though separate from the English plantations, were located in a cluster in close proximity to the English ones. All one hundred and eighty plantations were located along the coastal area between the Cassipora creek, nowadays known as Joden Savanne, and Torarica, approximately 40 km south of Paramaribo (see Figure 1.1 on page 4).

In 1667, the Dutch, led by Abraham Crijnssen, conquered Suriname during the second Anglo-Dutch War of 1665 to 1667. According to Hoefte (1998), this war began because England attempted to terminate the Dutch dominance over world trade routes. On July 31, 1667, via the peace treaty of Breda, Suriname was ceded to the Dutch in exchange for New Amsterdam, which is present day New York (Kaufman & Macpherson 2005). Consequently, as allowed under the

Figure 1.1: Location of plantations in late 17th century Suriname. Source: Mogge (1677)

conventions of the Treaty of Breda (Great Britain House of Lords 1761: 617–618), most of the English planters with enslaved Africans purchased before the cession to the Dutch, alongside indentured servants and free Whites, began leaving the mainland colony between 1668 and 1675 (Arbell 2002; Faber 1998; Godfrey & Godfrey 1995).

What was the linguistic situation while the English were in control of the colony? How did this linguistic situation change with the arrival and subsequent settlement of the Portuguese? What happened after the departure of the English and arrival of the Dutch and how did these social and linguistic changes contribute to the development of Sranan Tongo?

1.2.2 A change in the linguistic ecology of Suriname

The English population in Suriname, up until the commencement of their departure after 1667, consisted of planters, free Whites and indentured servants who were coming from Barbados (Arbell 2002; Sainsbury 1880). During the period of English control, specifically between the period 1650 to 1664, i.e. the period prior to the introduction of the Portuguese element into the colony, indentured servants from within the British Isles constituted the bulk of the population in the English colonies (Kenny 2006; Powell 2005; Armitage 2005). This is linguistically significant because these indentured servants "formed the primary [English Superstrate] linguistic models" (Arends 2002: 117) for the enslaved Africans with whom they worked side by side on the plantations (Galenson 2002).

According to Rens (1953), among the settlers going to Suriname from Barbados, some might have previously been residents of St. Kitts. This, according to Arends (2002: 117), is very significant because St. Kitts was not only the first colony to be colonised by the English, but it "... may [also] have been the centre of diffusion of restructured English throughout the Caribbean, including Barbados." It seems that it is for this reason that Arends (2002) holds the view that the English roots of the Surinamese English-lexicon creoles should not be sought in Barbados but in St. Kitts. I agree with Arends (2002) to an extent. However, given the migration patterns of indentured labourers from England during the period in which Suriname was settled, I would argue that ssA's English linguistic influence is a combination of St. Kitts' "restructured English", alongside the linguistic influence(s) from the indentured servants who arrived in Barbados during the early 1650s onwards (see Chapter 6).

The linguistic ecology of Suriname changed after 1664 with the arrival of the Portuguese Jews, who established their plantations in close proximity to the English ones. The subsequent linguistic situation had an effect on the ssA creole languages albeit in varying degrees (see Table 1.1). According to Rens (1953), the "Neger-English" that was spoken in the colony by both the English and enslaved Africans went through a process of fusion with the Portuguese linguistic systems that the Portuguese Jews and the enslaved took with them to Suriname.

The linguistic ecology in Suriname changed again in 1667 with the cession of the colony by the English to the Dutch. Barring runaway slaves, some of whom spoke "Neger-English" and the few English who had stayed, with most of the English indentured servants, planters and "Neger-English"-speaking enslaved Africans leaving the colony, Suriname's linguistic ecology soon changed to one dominated by Portuguese and Dutch. Intriguingly, "as far as the lexicons of the Surinamese Creoles are concerned, it is an undisputed fact that English ... [had] ... played a major role in their composition" (Arends 2002: 117). Irrespective of the Portuguese and Dutch linguistic influences from 1667 onwards, the English element was so deeply entrenched in the SSA creole languages that even to date they can still be classified as English-lexicon creole languages; this is illustrated in Table 1.1 below.

Table 1.1: Lexical sources of the 200-word basic vocabulary list for SSA

	English	Portuguese	Dutch	West African
Sranan	71.40%	3.70%	17.85%	1.59%
Aukan	76.47%	5.04%	15.97%	2.52%
Saramaccan	49.96%	34.88%	10.45%	4.74%

Table 1.1 does more than highlight the significance of the English element based on a look at the 200-word basic vocabulary for the SSA creole languages; the table also highlights the fact that Dutch had little linguistic influence on the SSA creole languages. This lack of significant linguistic influence from Dutch is possibly attributable to the fact that the Dutch were never able to implement, with any degree of success, the system of indentured servitude that the British were able to establish (Buddingh 1995). Added to this is the fact that even though Dutch became the official language of the colony and the "language of literacy after emancipation," it was a language of high status that was seldom used to communicate with speakers of Sranan (whether enslaved Africans or any of the English who were in the country) during the 17th and 18th century (Healy 1993: 279).

The table also highlights another interesting fact, i.e. that the Portuguese element, based on the 200-word basic vocabulary list, is far greater in Saramaccan than the other two ssa creoles. This has led some linguists, such as Perl (1995), to suggest that Saramaccan should be classified as a Portuguese-lexicon creole language. Though this is not a position that I hold, this current work is not the medium through which to contest this claim. Let us therefore move to a brief discussion of the linguistic development of ssa.

1.2.3 Linguistic development of ssa

There are a number of elaborate explanations that various linguists have provided concerning the development of the ssa creole languages. This dissertation does not concern itself with which of these explanations is more valid and/or trustworthy. For this reason, the discussion hereafter is but a brief presentation of a few of them.

There are two major hypotheses that attempt to account for the development of the ssa creole languages; these are the Parallel Origin Hypothesis and the Serial Origin hypothesis (Smith & Veenstra 2001). According to the Parallel Origin Hypothesis, Proto-Sranan, Proto-Saramaccan and Proto-Aukan developed independently, albeit from some type of Caribbean Plantation Pidgin English, hereafter CPPE, which might have existed in the English colonies during the first generation of slavery (Smith & Veenstra 2001; McWhorter 1998). CPPE possibly originated from an English pidgin that might have been developed and spoken by castle slaves along the West African slave settlements (McWhorter 2000).

According to McWhorter (2000), since all Atlantic English Creoles "... must trace to a single ancestor, it is most likely that the pidgin was transported to ... St. Kitts and Barbados [which were]... the first colonies settled [by the English] and the source of settlers and slaves to subsequent [English] colonies ..." (111). This transported English pidgin was possibly the same "... embryonic Medium for Inter-ethnic Communication ..." which according to Baker (1998: 347) existed in 1620s St. Kitts long before it became a first language and was spread to the other English territories. In all likelihood CPPE is the same as Baker's proposed mixed Afro-English communication system (Baker 1998), which was spread to the other British colonies including Suriname; CPPE might also be a further developed version of Baker's Medium for Inter-ethnic Communication (Baker 1998), which developed due to the influence of the indentured servants coming into the colonies from the 1650s onwards (see Chapter 6).

The Serial Origin hypothesis also attributes the development of ssa to CPPE. However, Proto-Sranan is considered to be the first to develop from CPPE, within Suriname, followed by Aukan and Saramaccan as offshoots from Sranan (Smith & Veenstra 2001; McWhorter 1998). Shortly after CPPE was transported to Suriname,

Sranan developed, before Saramaccan and Aukan, due to the continual contact between enslaved Africans, "... indentured servants and poor whites, who acted as bookkeepers and overseers on the plantations ..." (Cassidy & Le Page 1967: xii). This English, indentured servant-based, linguistic influence would certainly have lasted only until just after 1668, with the departure of the English.

Smith (2009; 2006; 2002) argued that Sranan developed in the first half of the 1660s. In fact, Smith (2009: 316) "... [dated] the creolization of Sranan at 1660–1665." This means that by the time of the arrival of the Portuguese Jews in 1664, Sranan or some semblance of it was already created. Smith's claim is supported by Rens (1953: 28) who claimed that prior to the arrival of the Portuguese Jews in Suriname, "Neger-English" had long been established among the enslaved Africans and white inhabitants of the country.

Sranan, by around 1680–1690, was partly relexified by Portuguese. This is attributed to the influence of Portuguese Jewish immigrants who were granted asylum in 1664 (McWhorter 2011; Smith 2006; Holm 1989). According to Smith (2008b: 156), these Portuguese Jews had brought "Portuguese speaking slaves with them to Suriname" when they first entered the then English colony. At some point there was a fusion of what Rens (1953) called Neger-Portuguese, spoken by the Portuguese enslaved Africans, and the Neger-English spoken by the English enslaved Africans and some of the indentured servants. This possibly took place during and after 1667, when the Portuguese Jews purchased Sranan (Neger-English) speaking enslaved Africans from the English who were preparing to migrate from Suriname due to its having been ceded to the Dutch (Ehrlich 2009; Mufwene 2001; Friedman 1999; McWhorter 1998; Wurm et al. 1996; Rens 1953). This fusion of the two languages saw the birth of a kind of Dju-Tongo (Jew language), a mixed Portuguese/English creole, in the middle of the Suriname River plantations (Arends et al. 1995).

By the 1690s, the first group of enslaved Africans ran away from the Portuguese Jewish plantations to form the first Saramaccan group in the interior of the country (Huber & Parkvall 1999). The high percentage of Portuguese lexical items in Saramaccan (see Table 1.1 on Page 6) is attributed to this Dju-Tongo, which according to Arends et al. (1995) "... [involved] the same mix of English, Portuguese and African elements as Saramaccan..." (169).

Aukan (commonly referred to as Ndjuka or Djuka) "... is lexically more similar to Sranan" (Huttar & Huttar 1994: Introduction). Huttar & Huttar (1994) claimed that this creole language variety appeared in the first half of the 18th century, when "large numbers of slaves escaped from plantations chiefly along the Cottica and Commewijne rivers where a contact language drawing much of its lexicon from English was in use" (Huttar & Huttar 1994: Introduction). This contact language is what McWhorter (1998) considered to be Sranan.

Since most of the English would have already migrated from Suriname by 1680, resulting in Sranan's linguistic ecology being one that was dominated by Portuguese and Dutch, how do we account for Aukan being similar to Sranan? How can we account for Sranan still being spoken as the lingua franca today, as opposed to Saramaccan or some Dutch-based creole that is a fusion of Dutch and Neger English (Sranan)? According to Holm (1994) the Dutch in Suriname treated Sranan as a language in its own right, though not one of prestige. Consequently, they learned it as a second language to communicate with their enslaved Africans, some of whom were acquired from the migrating English after Suriname?s cession to the Dutch (see Chapter 6).

This work does not attempt to settle which of the two hypotheses, i.e. the Parallel Origin Hypothesis or the Serial Origin Hypothesis, is more trustworthy. What is important is the fact that ssA, specifically Sranan, contains what might be considered "fossilized" linguistic remnants of an early English colonial period. Therefore, it is being proposed here, that these linguistic "fossils" can be used to trace the dialect origin(s), in England, of the early English influence.

1.3 The problem

Though linguists, such as Smith (2008a; 1987) and Mufwene (2008a; 2001), present 17th century dialects of English as the lexical input for English creoles, Smith was more specific regarding the nature of this input. He posited dialect levelling involving an approximation of an emerging 17th century "... London English, primarily Standard Early Modern English ..." (Smith 2008a: 118). He held this view because he believed that "... the English that developed in the general London area [was] ancestral to all forms of English developed external to the British Isles ..." (Smith 2008a: 118). He supported this claim by tracing systematic sound changes based on south-east England English input and their realisations in Suriname. Smith (2008a; 1987) did not, however, present evidence to repudiate the possibility of a pan-dialectal account of origin, i.e. the possibility that the origin of this influence was coming from dialects from all over England. This latter view is endorsed by Mufwene (2008a; 2001).

Mufwene (2008a; 2001) believed that "... the target for those who made the creoles, consisted of several non-standard [dialect] varieties [of the European lexifiers that were] competing with each other ..." (Mufwene 2008a: 21). Like Smith (2008a; 1987), Mufwene (2008a; 2001) failed to provide any assessment of the possibility of an alternative account to his pan-dialectal one; i.e. he did not address the possibility of a mono-dialectal source of origin, such as that proposed by Smith (2008a; 1987).

1.4 Significance of research

This research attempts to settle the pan-dialectal and the mono-dialectal contention surrounding the nature of the historical lexico-phonetic input in English creoles, specifically Sranan. To this end, it puts forward a methodological apparatus that one can use to undertake such reconstructive work and achieve replicable results. This methodological tool involves a combination of statistics (Chapter 4), English dialect geography (Chapter 5) and 17th century history of England (Chapter 6).

1.5 Outline of chapters

Chapter 2, *Brief overview: Views on superstrate influence*, begins with a brief discussion of the theories of creole genesis that exist to date. The discussion then looks specifically at two superstratist approaches of origin which offer opposing ideas about the nature of the superstrate input; it then focuses specifically on the superstrate influence in Sranan. The discussion concludes with an explanation and rationale for the direction that this research takes in attempting to establish what Sranan's linguistic influence from England looks like and how best to account for it.

Chapter 3, *About the data and research design*, is divided into two major sections. The first section, *Data Sources*, is a discussion and presentation of the Sranan, the English of England, 17th century history of England data sources and the linguistic features assessed in this research. The second section, *Research Design*, is a detailed discussion and presentation of:

  a. the approach taken in gathering, organising and using the English regional dialect data and the Sranan data; and

  b. the processes that took place at each stage of the proposed tripartite methodological model used to undertake this research.

Chapter 4, *Testing probability of origin*, is a presentation of the statistical component of the methodological apparatus at work, using 45 putative lexico-phonetic English etyma, hereafter the SED45, which have been selected for this research (see Chapter 3). The chapter discusses the probability of finding a single dialect locality of origin, which exhibits a high degree of correspondence between the 45 putative input etyma and their Sranan reflexes, hereafter referred to as the Sranan45. It then looks at the significance of actually finding a single such locality of origin from within England and subsequently presents the actual results of the statistical analysis.

Chapter 5, *A dialect geography approach*, is a presentation and discussion of potential locations of origin in England of the English reflexes for the Sranan45. In this chapter, the results of the statistical analysis presented in Chapter 4 are temporarily disregarded and the data are analysed anew within a dialect geography framework. This involves plotting on a map of England the geo-linguistic distribution of the SED45 etyma. The chapter concludes with a discussion of the degree of corroboration between the results of the geo-linguistic mapping and the results of the statistical analysis of the SED45.

Chapter 6, *The historical complement*, is a discussion of the 17th century migration patterns of people from England going to British colonies in the Americas. The focus of the discussion is on the patterns of migration from the locations identified via the statistical analysis and the geo-linguistic mapping as the potential sources for the Sranan45. The discussion is concerned with answering three main questions that are posed at the end of Chapter 5. These are as follows:

1. Can we establish a chain of migration from England to Suriname, between the periods 1650–1667?

2. Can we establish a chain of migration from England, within the same time span mentioned in (1), to the English colonies in the Caribbean and subsequently Suriname?

3. Can we, if the answer(s) to (1) and/or (2) is/are in the affirmative, then determine what percentage of the total number of migrants to the Caribbean, including Suriname, is from the localities pinpointed in Chapters 4 and 5?

Chapter 7, *A Tale of Two Dialect Inputs*, is a discussion of the composite findings from the three components of the analytical tool (see Chapters 4–6). This final chapter also looks at the significance of these combined findings as they relate to Sranan, Linguistic reconstruction, Dialect geography, Creole and Historical Linguistics and English-lexicon creole languages in general.

2 Brief overview: Views on superstrate influence

2.1 "Creole": The people

An online search for additional literature, to add to those already sourced for this research, concerning superstrate and creole languages respectively, led to an article entitled *The Context of Wide Sargasso Sea > Social/Political Context > Creole Identity and Language.*[1] This article presented a discussion about the social and political context in relation to Creole identity and language in the novel Wide Sargasso Sea. The novel, written by Dominican-born author Jean Rhys, which is set in the 1966 postcolonial era, told the story of heiress Antoinette Cosway. The article mentioned the fact that the term "Creole" was originally used to refer to Whites of British (like Rhys' Antoinette) and/or of other European parentage, who were born in the Caribbean. A subsequent read of Page's (1997) review of Wide Sargasso Sea highlighted the following:

> [Antoinette] … is descended from the plantation owners, and her father has had many children by Negro women. She can be accepted neither by the Negro community nor by the representatives of the colonial centre. As a white creole she is nothing. The taint of racial impurity, coupled with the suspicion that she is mentally imbalanced brings about her inevitable downfall ….

Confronted, again, by the concept of "White Creole", there was a need to find out more about this concept and this led to the works of Saxon (1989) and Ward (2004). Both works expressed the fact that in New Orleans, for example, the term "Creole" provoked two distinct responses. The first response was that Creoles were children of "… European parents born in a French or Spanish colony" (Saxon 1989: 270). The second response was that the term refers to "someone whose ancestors came to the colonies from France or Spain, who was born in Louisiana,

---

[1]http://crossref-it.info/textguide/Wide-Sargasso-Sea/29/1915, last accessed on November 12, 2018.

and who may be light-skinned and black as well" (Ward 2004: xiv). However, the Creoles who gave the first response, would never agree with the last half of the second response, i.e. that Creoles can be "light-skinned and black". This is despite the fact that their own ancestors "... fathered mixed-race children" with Black slave paramours (Ward 2004: xiv).

The term "Creole", when it is applied to Whites, such as Rhys's Antoinette, most often refers to rich, upper class, and land-owning descendants of Europeans, who were born in the Americas (see Cassidy 1982). These White Creoles, by virtue of the fact that their nannies, playmates and servants were most often enslaved Africans, spoke a creole language such as Sranan (Cassidy 1982). However, the main focus of this research is not on this group of people. Instead, the focus is on the speech of poor Whites, these being the indentured servants who came to the Caribbean colonies. These poor Whites and their descendants, who came to exist in socially isolated communities, preserved to varying extents the language forms of their British forefathers (see Aceto 2010 and Williams 2003).

Apart from the use of the term "Creole" in reference to "pure" (unmixed) Whites of Caribbean origin, the line "... As a white creole she is nothing ..." stood out to me. It made me wonder about the language of these White Creoles, and also of the poor Whites, who in large numbers migrated to the colonies as indentured servants (see Chapter 6). According to historians such as Galenson (2002), it was common practice for enslaved Africans and white indentured servants to work side-by-side on plantations. This sociolinguistic situation represented a perfect scenario for intense language contact. Black speech in Caribbean had been widely studied but had Creole linguists ever thought to study the language of these poor Whites? The answer to this question was yes, but not to any significant degree. According to Williams (2003), early research of this kind had been "hindered by a lack of knowledge of "white" dialects ... [and] ... the work that has been done has generally suffered from a lack of understanding of the social and cultural dynamics of "whiteness" in Anglophone West Indian contexts" (Williams 2003: 95).

How would the findings of this research relate to the body of research on the language of the descendants of these poor Whites? This was one of three important questions to address whilst tackling the three research questions presented in Chapter 1 (see Chapter 7 for the remaining two questions). In Chapter 7, I compare the findings from the contemporary works of Aceto (2010), Williams (2003), Blake (2004) and others, and the significance of their work within the context of my findings. These linguists researched what Trudgill (2002: 30) referred to as the "lesser-known varieties of English". These are a set of relatively unstudied, native varieties of English that are spoken in some parts of the English-speaking world (Trudgill 2002). What is the language spoken by the descendants of these poor Whites? Is it English, or a "Caribbeanized" dialect of English? In most cases, it is the same or similar to the linguistic code used by Blacks (see Cassidy 1982).

2.2 "Creole" language and theories of genesis

What exactly are "creole" languages and how are they formed? McWhorter, in his work *Defining Creole* (McWhorter 2005), expressed the fact that after years of established Creole Language Studies, no consensus had yet been reached as to what a creole really is. Defining this concept, according to McWhorter (2005), was/is such a sensitive issue that some researchers felt it best to leave it alone. Notwithstanding the challenge involved in defining the term "creole", various linguists, such as Kihm (1980) and Chaudenson (1992), used the word as a socio-historical term "referring to certain languages born as lingua francas amidst heavy contact between two or more languages" (McWhorter 2005: 9). This definition is an example of one of three main types of definitions that Hickey (1997) claimed to have identified within the field of Creole Linguistics. He classified these three types as "External", "Acquisitional" and "Structural".

An External definition, such as that presented above, considers factors outside of the language itself; a "creole" is therefore defined based on its sociolinguistic historical context of development. Acquisitional definitions identify creoles as language varieties that arose in situations where a generation of speakers developed these languages from significantly reduced and imperfectly acquired colonial lexifiers. Structural definitions identify creoles as languages that have undergone reformation with respect to their lexifier language(s) and possibly substrate languages (Hickey 1997).

These definitional types originated from the various theories of genesis that had been presented for the various languages labelled "creoles". These theories can be grouped together according to those that focus on the influence of European lexifiers, those that focus on non-European influence, and those that regard "... universals of language acquisition and/or language-internal development as the crucial factor in creole genesis" (Braun 2009: 3). As with the three categories of definitions for "creole" highlighted by Hickey (1997), the theories of creole genesis can be grouped into three main types. The more contemporary versions of these are briefly presented hereafter, under the headings *Eurocentric theories of creole genesis, Non-Eurocentric theories of creole genesis* and *Language universal theories of creole genesis*. The presentation of these approaches is followed by a discussion of where all three types of approaches converge.

2.2.1 Eurocentric theories of creole genesis

Theories that regard the impact of European influences as being the most vital to creole formation, range for example, from the early works of Bloomfield (1933), Hall (1966), Ferguson (1971), to the more recent works of Chaudenson (1992), and Mufwene (2001; 2008a,b). The core principle of Eurocentric theories of genesis is that creoles are approximations of their European lexifiers (Baker 2000: 43). Mufwene (2008a), for instance, suggested that "in all ... cases of language evolution, the action of competition among competing ... systems is evident " (Mufwene 2008a: 58). Furthermore, in language contact settings involving one target language (the lexifier), with the other language(s) involved offering some competition, "... learners ... normally approximate the pattern provided by speakers of the target language" (Mufwene 2008a: 122). The same is claimed to be true for those socio-historical contact situations that resulted in the linguistic systems referred to as "creoles".

In these situations, i.e. those leading to the formation of "creoles", Europeans and non-Europeans interacted regularly and since non-Europeans had no one with whom to use their own ethnic language(s), the features of the founder populations, i.e. of the European language, had the advantage in the majority of their linguistic forms being selected over non-European ones (Mufwene 1996b). One effect of this was that children born into such situations, and also their parents, might not have seen knowledge of such non-European languages as particularly necessary (Mufwene 2008b). In fact, this might be one of the major reasons why "... structural features of creoles ... [are seemingly] ... predetermined to a large extent (though not exclusively) by characteristics of the vernaculars spoken by the populations that founded the colonies in which they developed" (Mufwene 1996b: 28). Mufwene's assertions, as with those of many other superstratists, were influenced by what (Braun 2009: 3) referred to "... as one of the much debated ... [Superstratist] ... approaches", i.e. Chaudenson's (Chaudenson 1992) theory of genesis.

According to Braun (2009), Chaudenson (1992) viewed creoles "as modifications of non-standard European superstrates with little influence from the native languages of the slaves" (Braun 2009: 3). Chaudenson (1992) asserted that when we closely examine how colonial societies got their start, we will see that "... the duration of the period during which Whites were more numerous than Blacks was considerable, and conditions did not change on the very day the black population outnumbered the white population..." (Chaudenson 1992: 60). Since this was the case, what he referred to as 'first generation creoles', such as Sranan, Jamaican, etc., would therefore be approximations of the European language(s) spoken by the Whites. This assertion was voiced from within his earlier work on French creoles in which he posited that these creoles, i.e. French-lexicon creoles, could be traced back to a particular French dialect spoken in 17th and 18th century France, i.e. the dialect that was in use in the Normandy region (Chaudenson 1979). Chaudenson (1979) claimed that there was no need for Blacks to outnumber the Whites for a creole to have developed. In fact, (French) creoles would have developed while the lexifier language was still relatively accessible. In such socio-linguistic conditions, where the Whites, who spoke vernacular French, still outnumbered the Blacks, these Blacks were no doubt motivated to abandon their native language(s) to be able to communicate with others (Chaudenson 1979).

In defence of his assertions, Chaudenson & Mufwene (2001) stated that even those theorists that advocate for a non-European focus in creole genesis all agree that "for the most part, creolization has occurred through collective, imperfect, and approximate "learning" of French (or, more generally, any other lexifier) ..." (Chaudenson & Mufwene 2001). The most extreme of these Non-Eurocentric theorists is Mervyn Alleyne, who in his *Comparative Afro-American* work (Alleyne 1980) claimed that the most essential language influences during the periods of creole geneses, specifically for English-lexicon creoles, were the Non-European (African) languages present in the colonies. This is discussed in the following section.

2.2.2 Non-Eurocentric theories of creole genesis

Non-Eurocentric accounts of origin, which are hereafter referred to simply as Substratist approaches, have their origin in the early 19th century works of philologists such as Baissac (1880). The essence of the Superstrate approaches is that "creole" languages owe much of their development to the influence of the African (substrate) language(s) that were present during the creole formation period. Mufwene (1990; 1996a) identified three main types of Substratist models: the first type, for which the proponents are Alleyne (1980; 1996) and Holm (1989), "identifies the source of individual features in diverse substrate languages... that must have been represented in the ethnolinguistic ecological setting of the relevant contact" (Mufwene 1996a: 167); the second type, endorsed by Lefebvre (1998; 2004) and Lumsden (1999), posited a process of "relexification", i.e. the replacement of L1 (substrate language) lexical items with their L2 (European) counterparts; the third type of substratist approach, endorsed by Keesing (1988), "... validates substrate influence with the relative typological homogeneity of languages in contact with the lexifier" (Mufwene 1996a: 167).

The substratist theory of creole genesis presented by Alleyne (1980) could be considered to be the most extreme of those highlighted in the previous paragraph (Byrne 1987). In fact, his account is in stark contrast to the most extreme superstratist approach (see §2.2.1). Alleyne (1980) asserted that the creole languages that he focused on (Atlantic English lexicon Creoles), in which he included the SSA creoles, are essentially a continuity of the African languages that went into their development. Alleyne supported his claim via the presentation of his observation that "... the rules which account for [serial verb constructions] are basically the same in... [the Atlantic Creoles] as in Kwa languages [African substrate]" (1980: 167) and that the characteristics of serialization in the Kwa languages "seem to be closer to Saramaccan than to other... [Atlantic Creole]... dialects" (Alleyne 1980: 167). Alleyne based most of his assumptions on the observations he made of Saramaccan, which in his view "... may represent the oldest layer of creole known to us..." and thus the least altered from its substrate (Alleyne 1979: 91).

The SSA creoles seemed to represent a haven for most creole linguistic study, including my own, given their peculiar differences from other English creoles, such as [kouru] for *cold* where others have [kuol]. These creoles were/are so favoured that even those theorists who advocate for linguistic universals, as opposed to (Non-)Eurocentric accounts, make reference to them, specifically Saramaccan, as "radical creoles" (cf. Bickerton 1977; 1981/2016; 1984; 1999). These radical creoles as expressed by Byrne (1987: 3) were so-called because "[their] ... grammars come closer to approximating the unmarked state of our innate, genetically endowed faculté de langage." Just as the Superstratist and Substratist schools had/have their most extreme advocates in the form of Chaudenson & Mufwene (2001) and Alleyne (1980), respectively, Bickerton (1977; 1981/2016; 1984; 1999) is the theorist most associated with Universalist theories of creole genesis.

2.2.3 Language universal theories of creole genesis

Bickerton's (1977; 1981/2016; 1984; 1999) Language (Universal) Bioprogram Hypothesis, hereafter LBH, asserted that creole languages, in particular Saramaccan, closely approximated, neither their superstrates nor their substrates but the inborn, genetically endowed, "faculté de langage" that all humans are born with (Bickerton 1984: 158). The importance and reliance in this 'faculty of language' is echoed in the work DeGraff (2001), who defined "creole" as "... the product of extraordinary external (sociohistorical) factors coupled with ordinary (internal) linguistic resources inherent to the human faculté de langage" (DeGraff 2001: 11).

Bickerton's (1977; 1981/2016; 1984; 1999) biological predisposition for language comes with certain preset features such as a natural tense-aspect schema that is embedded in certain neural pathways of the brain (Bickerton 1975). In his own words, Bickerton (1981/2016: 2) stated the following: "... all members of our species are born with a bioprogram for language which can function in the absence of adequate input."

Bickerton's (1977; 1981/2016; 1984; 1999) hypothesis seemingly paralleled particular components of Superstratist theories. The reasons for making this assertion are found in the following aspects of Bickerton's (1977; 1981/2016; 1984; 1999) theory of the genesis of creole languages, specifically English creole languages:

1. European plantation owners in need of a large-scale labour force imported enslaved Africans to work for them. Consequently, pidginization of these European languages took place. This pidginization process was in essence second-language learning, characterized by limited access to, and therefore inadequate acquisition of, the European lexifier languages (Bickerton 1977). This, of course, resulted in the demise of the African languages which had little or no part to play in the process.

2. Children born into these multi-linguistic ecologies, whilst learning these relatively unstable pidgins (Bickerton 1977: 49) as their first languages, "[received] ... restrictive input ..." and for this reason their built-in grammars, which are conditioned by the bioprogram, were triggered, and continued into adulthood (cf. Bickerton 1979; 1984; 1981/2016). Whilst all this was occurring, the adults' linguistic repertoires, with more and more access to the European lexifiers, were also developing. These adults were moving away from both their L1s (native languages) and a soon-to-be obsolete and extremely flexible pidgin (Bickerton 1981/2016). Creole languages were the linguistic outcome of these two co-occurring events.

The LBH, however, disregarded the creole languages of the descendants of "White Creoles" and poor White indentured servants (see Schumann 1783; Cassidy 1982), which were/are spoken in Suriname and around the English world (see Trudgill 2002).

2.2.4 Where all theories of creole genesis concur

What is evident from the discussions presented in §2.2.1 to §2.2.3 is that the typological classification of creoles is a major long-standing issue for Creole linguists, and though several theories of genesis have been proposed, it seems that one

agreed upon theory of origin might never be found. Notwithstanding, all theorists, including those discussed in the previous sections, agree that in most cases
the majority of the lexical entries in "creoles" are derived from their lexifier languages, more specifically from 17th century regional dialects of their European
lexifier languages (Chaudenson 1992; Chaudenson & Mufwene 2001; Mufwene
1996b; 2008a; Lefebvre 2004; McWhorter 2005). Of these theorists, two seminal
works from within the same theoretical school of thought, i.e. the Superstratist
camp, provided me with varying theories regarding the nature of this Superstrate
lexical influence. These were Mufwene's (2001; 2008a) 'All-the-dialects view', referred to hereafter as the pan-dialectal account, and Chaudenson's (1979; 1992;
2001) 'Single-dialect view', hereafter the mono-dialectal account.

2.2.4.1 The mono-dialectal account

Chaudenson's (1979) work, as mentioned in §2.2.1, addressed French creoles, specifically those spoken in and around the Indian Ocean. He was able to show that
the linguistic features noticed in these creoles could be traced back to a particular
17th to 18th century French dialect spoken in Normandy (Western France). Chaudenson did a detailed comparison of the structural correspondences between
various French Creole reflexes and their French dialectal etyma. The assertion
that French creoles were genetically derived from 17th to 18th century French
was asserted from within the early works of Hall (1953), and Goodman (1964),
whereas Chaudenson (1979) was the first to pinpoint a precise dialect of French
from which this influence could be said to have originated.

2.2.4.2 The pan-dialectal account

Mufwene's (2001) pan-dialectal account described a creole's lexical influence as
being made up of "... composite varieties from among diverse dialects of the same
language ..." (p. 3). This account provided a counter thesis to Chaudenson's account of Superstrate influence. According to Mufwene (2008a), "... the target for
those who made the creoles consisted of several non-standard varieties [of the
17th and 18th century European lexifier languages that were] competing with
each other..." (p. 21). These dialects developed into a new colonial dialect that
preserved at its core a mixture of common features found across the diverse
dialects of the lexifier language. These competing features were thrown into a
pan-dialectal "feature pool", thereby becoming accessible for selection by colonial speech communities (Mufwene 2008a; 2001). Survival of these features was
ensured if they were more frequent, more salient, and/or more transparent than

other alternatives. Survival was also guaranteed if a competing feature appeared in one of the other languages present during the creole formation period, for example one or more of the West African languages (Mufwene 2001).

2.2.4.3 The pan-dialectal account vs. the mono-dialectal Account

There is a possibility that Chaudenson is right as it relates to French-lexicon creole languages and Mufwene is equally right about English-lexicon creole languages. However, there is also the possibility that a Chaudenson-type approach might better account for the nature of the English input in English-lexicon creoles. Since this is the case one of the questions that this research attempted to answer is which of the two accounts, i.e. Chaudenson's Mono-dialectal account or Mufwene's pan-dialectal account, better explains the nature and origin of the lexical and phonetic input in Sranan. To this end, this work refrains from focusing on the debate surrounding when, or how, what we know as modern Sranan was formed. Instead, using some of the oldest and most available secondary Sranan data, an attempt was made to reconstruct and trace the 17th century putative English input that would have influenced the Surinamese proto-language that soon developed into Proto-Sranan and the two other SSA creoles, i.e. Proto-Saramaccan and Proto-Aukan. In so doing an attempt was made to investigate whether there were multiple dialectal inputs from all over England or a single dialectal input from within a specific region.

2.2.5 The search for Sranan's English dialectal influence

One seminal work, which addressed the Superstrate origins of the Surinamese English creoles, is Smith's (1987), *The genesis of the creole languages of Surinam*. In this work Smith used Historical Phonology and attempted to reconstruct the linguistic shape and origin of SSA's 17th century European input. Smith (1987: 6), utilising knowledge of "... seventeenth century English and Portuguese..." alongside 18th and 19th century SSA data sources, attempted to find and discuss the correspondences between them. Smith's (1987) major concern was the origin and "linguistic interrelationships" between SSA's lexical and phonological influences, i.e. English, Dutch and Portuguese.

Smith's (1987) work, like Mufwene's (2001), points to 17th century regional dialects of English as the input for English Creoles. However, similar to Chaudenson (1979), Smith (1987) was more explicit about the nature of SSA's English input. He proposed 'Standard Early Modern London English', with some input from regional non-standard dialects around London, as the main input for SSA (Smith

2008a; 1987). Given Smith's proposed "London English" account of origin, along-side determining whether a mono-dialectal account or a pan-dialectal account of origin can best explain Sranan's English Superstrate origin, one of the other major issues that this research also addressed was whether Smith's proposal is trustworthy. What this meant was that, in trying to determine whether the English dialectal influence in Sranan was from a composite of dialects (Mufwene 2008a; 2001) from all over England, or a single regional dialect, there was also an attempt to determine whether Smith's proposed "London-English" was the only source of Sranan's English linguistic influence. In doing so, Smith's (1987) work was taken as a stepping stone for this current research. However, whereas Smith's (1987) work focussed on determining in a more general way the European origins (from Portuguese, Dutch and English) of Sranan's lexical and phonetic influences, this current research focussed solely on the English dialectal influence(s) from within England in a bid to find the dialect or dialects from within England that were of linguistic influence.

In a perfect world where things are as plain as "black and white", and shades of "grey" are non-existent, an agreed upon definition of "creole" exists and the answers to all questions surrounding "creole" would have already been found. Sadly, this is not that perfect world; however, whatever the term "creole", in reference to language, means to the various researchers in the field of Creole Linguistics, it is generally accepted that Sranan is a creole language. This being the case, in taking Smith's (1987) work as a stepping stone (see Chapter 3), a tri-partite methodological model was created to determine the dialectal origin(s), in England, of those lexical and phonetic influences that needed to be present during the formation of this creole language. The components of this methodological model are discussed in the following chapter. This model consists of statistical analysis, Dialect Geography techniques and analysis of 17th century England migration history. As will become evident in the following chapters, the rationale behind using this methodological model is that it allowed for triangulation of results from three diverse types of analyses. Such corroboration of the results across all three types of analyses meant a higher degree of trustworthiness. This model and the data that were used in this research are discussed in greater detail in the following chapter.

3 About the data and research design

3.1 Introduction

This research had two chief aims. The first aim was to develop a novel tripartite methodological analysis tool, with which the second aim could be addressed. The second aim involved an attempt to bring an end to the contention surrounding the origin of the English lexico-phonetic element in Sranan; i.e. whether this origin was best explained by a pan-dialectal account of origin, or a mono-dialectal account of origin. In attempting to accomplish the above-mentioned aims, the research relied heavily on three types of secondary data. These were Sranan data, English dialect geography data and historical data surrounding 17th century migration from England to the Caribbean and South America.

3.2 Data sources

3.2.1 Sranan data

The main source of data on Sranan that was used to conduct this research was the *Dictionary of Sranan Tongo* (Wilner 2007; 2003; 1992). This was supplemented by four complementary sources in the form of the wordlists of Stichting Volkslectuur (Stichting 1980), Schumann (1783), Von Fermin (1769), and Herlein (1718). Because of the varying periods in which the four wordlists and dictionary were compiled, the spelling conventions used across them varied considerably. The phone [u], for example, was represented as ⟨oe⟩ in Stichting Volkslectuur (Stichting 1980) but as ⟨u⟩ in Wilner (2003). The ⟨oe⟩ form used in Stichting Volkslectuur (Stichting 1980) is possibly Dutch-based, whereas the ⟨u⟩ used in Wilner (2003) is possibly based on the International Phonetic Alphabet (IPA).

Two steps were taken to deal with this issue of variability across the Sranan data sources. First, Smith's historical phonology work, *The Genesis of the Creole Languages of Surinam* (Smith 1987), was used to help reconstruct the actual phones that each writing convention was representing. Smith (1987) provided a very systematic and detailed discussion of how to interpret the phonetic information behind the graphemes in each of the wordlists. For the purpose of uniformity, the phonetic forms that these graphemes represented were then transcribed in accordance with the conventions of the revised 2005 IPA. Second, where there was a variation in the lexico-phonetic shape of a word found across these sources, preference was given to the oldest variant; the oldest variant was selected because the aim was to work with items that would represent, as much as possible, what Sranan might have looked like in the 17th century. This was an important step since the intention was to compare not just the lexical form but also phonetic composition of Sranan words and their potential English etyma. Accordingly, the English dialectal data, discussed in §3.2.2, were also transcribed using the above-mentioned revised IPA convention.

3.2.2 English dialect data

> Rarely are the characteristics of a language uniform across the region where it is used. Internal spatial variations in a linguistic region are called dialects, and language geographers study these variations in an effort to distinguish and understand the geographic qualities of dialect use ... (Hanks 2011: 209).

Dialect geographies shed light on lexical, phonological, syntactic and morphological diversity of individual languages over geographic spaces. These works allow linguists to generate linguistic atlases, i.e. maps that sectionalise a particular geographic space according to dialectal differences and similarities, as opposed to geographic and/or political boundaries. The importance of English dialect geography to this work was twofold. First, it provided lexical and phonetic dialectal data for the English etyma relevant to the Sranan reflexes of English origin. Second, it allowed for the identification of the potential regional dialectal variants and sources for these items.

There are four main dialect geographies for the English dialects spoken in the British Isles. These are: the *Survey of Anglo-Welsh Dialects* (Parry 1977; 1979) and Penhallurick (1991), the *Linguistic Survey of Scotland* (Mather & Speitel 1975), *A Sound Atlas of Irish English* (Hickey 2004) and the *Survey of English Dialects* (Orton et al. 1962–71).

The Survey of Anglo-Welsh Dialects "... is the most comprehensive collection of Welsh English data ... [archived] at the Department of English, University of Wales, Swansea..." This collection of Welsh data is attributed to two researchers. The first is David Parry, under whose supervision "... material was collected in rural areas of Wales between 1968 and 1982 ... and in urban areas between 1985 and 1987 (Penhallurick 2004: 100). The second researcher is Robert Penhallurick who, in 1991, carried out a survey in the north of Wales, specifically to collect data on the conservative rural English dialect spoken in the counties of Gwynedd and Clwyd (Penhallurick 1991).

The Linguistic Survey of Scotland, which was undertaken by Mather & Speitel (1975), does not necessarily qualify as dialect geography. The data contained in this work was the result of a postal questionnaire survey that, according to Macaulay (1977: 225), suffered from a "... loss of phonological information..." and also from fundamental design flaws in how the sample population was selected. Head teachers from across Scotland, as opposed to trained researchers, were instructed to hand out some of the questionnaires to "... middle-aged or older ... life-long inhabitants..." in their districts (Macaulay 1977: 14).

Henry (1958) in his "Preliminary Report" outlined proposals to develop a dialect geography of Irish English. His preliminary objectives were not achieved and the result was only a minute collection of word charts from within the agricultural sphere (Corrigan 2010). There is however, contemporary work that was produced by Hickey (2004), which was built on over 1,500 anonymous vernacular samples, audio recorded from 1,200 informants across rural and metropolitan settings in all thirty-two counties in Ireland (Corrigan 2010; Hickey 2004). Hickey's *A Sound Atlas of Irish English* was created to provide a present-day depiction of Irish English, specifically as it related to the language use of the younger generation of Irish English speakers (Hickey 2004).

The final dialect geography, the *Survey of English Dialects*, hereafter SED, was undertaken by Orton et al. (1962–71) between 1962 and 1971, via audio recorded sessions done by trained researchers, using an orally administered questionnaire. The questionnaire consisted of "... 1,322 questions of which 387 are for phonological, 128 for morphological, and 77 for syntactical purposes [respectively], the remaining 730 being mainly concerned with the lexicon" (Orton & Dieth 1962: 15).

History tells us that immigrants to the 17th century English colonies came from Ireland, Scotland, Wales and England. However, the aim was to pinpoint Sranan's earliest English input and for this reason the study focused only on identifying Sranan's early English dialectal origin(s) from within England. There are a number of reasons for having only dealt with 17th century England. As noted earlier, some of these included the fact that major Irish and Scottish migration to the American colonies did not occur until the late 18th century, i.e. 1718–1785 for the Irish (Griffin 2001) and 1716 for the Scots (see Dobson 2005), respectively. By these periods Suriname was no longer an English held colony, having already been ceded to the Dutch in 1667. Also, there were issues of comparability between the dialect geographies. *The Sound Atlas of Irish English*, for example, only provided present day Irish English data as opposed to more archaic versions of this language (Hickey 2004); the Scottish English dialect geography could not be classified as a dialect geography proper and it did not provide phonological data from which cross-dialectal comparisons could be made. Also, according to Macaulay (1977), it suffered from fundamental design flaws in the selection of the sample population; untrained data collectors, i.e. head teachers from across Scotland were instructed to hand out some of the questionnaires to "... middle-aged or older ... life-long inhabitants..." in their districts (Macaulay 1977: 14), there was no means by which to determine whether the teachers themselves did not fill out some of the questionnaires. In addition, the historical literature indicated that of the migrants to the American colonies during the period in which Suriname was a British colony, i.e. 1650–1667, the vast majority came from within the southwestern England counties of Somerset, Gloucestershire, Wiltshire and Monmouthshire (Burg 1995; Schaefer 1998), the latter being a Welsh county bordering Herefordshire and Gloucestershire to the west, which was also surveyed in the SED (see §3.2.2.1).

The fact that Irish English, Scottish English and Welsh English dialects formed a part of the input in English-based Creoles of the Americas (Mufwene 2001; Smith 1987) cannot be downplayed. However, for the above-mentioned reasons The *Survey of English Dialects* was the main dialect geography source used in this research.

3.2.2.1 The survey of English dialects

Orton & Dieth (1962) held traditional regional English dialects as being best preserved by farming communities, and as such "... the questionnaire [used in the SED, was] constructed for the farmer" (Orton & Dieth 1962: 44). Since this was the case, the questions asked dealt mainly with "... husbandry, home life and nature... [and areas such as] ... fishing, mining, weaving... [were] ... excluded as being too technical and not universal" (Orton & Dieth 1962: 44). Orton believed that responses to questions of the above-mentioned types "... would [have] shed light on the lexical, phonological and morphological diversity of spoken English" (Leads Archive of Vernacular Culture (LAVC)).

The SED was conducted in 313 localities across England and parts of Wales. This also included two localities in the Isle of Man. The localities in Wales were surveyed because they border localities in the west of England (Orton et al. 1962–71) and dialects of Welsh English in this region were influenced by south-west England English speakers, who migrated across the Bristol Channel from Somersetshire and Devon, from as early as the 12th century (Penhallurick 2004). Also, what we call Wales and England are political terms (Nicholas 1872), as opposed

to linguistic ones. Consequently, political lines indicated on a map do not correspond to actual physical boundaries, such as mountains, which separate people
who live in localities that border each other. In other words, what is spoken in a
given region is not determined by how that region is politically divided (Orton
et al. 1962–71).

According to Orton & Dieth (1962), the localities were selected according to
their "... geographical isolativity and relativity to each other... [with] ... preference given to agricultural communities that had a fairly stable population of
about 500 inhabitants for a century or so" (Orton & Dieth 1962: 15). The survey
was geared towards eliciting archaic, "lexical features... in the form of ... phonological variants... and grammatical features" (Orton & Dieth 1962: 45). Since this
was their goal, the researchers took as their target population "... men and wom-
en, sixty and over..." (Orton & Dieth 1962: 45) because they were considered to
be more likely to best preserve the traditional dialect.

The SED was to be published in five parts under the headings (A): Introduction,
(B): Basic Material, (C): Selected Incidental Material, (D): Linguistic Atlas of England and (E): Phonetic Transcriptions, of the audio recorded interviews (Orton &
Dieth 1962). However, to date, only parts (A), (B) and (D) can be found in print,
because after the publication of the basic material and possibly due to the death
of Orton in 1975, neither Parts (C) nor (E) were published.

Part (D) was itself not published as a single atlas at first, "but in the form of
six, often parallel and overlapping atlases ... the earliest of these [being] Kolb's
(Kolb 1979)' *Atlas of English Sounds*" (Fischer & Ammann 1991: 12). Orton's originally envisioned Linguistic Atlas of England was not published until 1978 and
in keeping with his (Orton's) original wish, it contained "... phonological, lexical,
morphological and syntactic maps..." based on the responses of the interviewees
that could be found in the Basic Material (Fischer & Ammann 1991: 12).

This current research relied heavily on Parts (A): Introduction, (B): Basic Material and (D): Linguistic Atlas of England. Part (A): Introduction contained an
index, referred to as the 'List of Key-words', which highlighted the particular
feature/variable that Orton & Dieth (1962) were attempting to capture from the
questions asked during the survey. This index indicated whether a particular fea-
ture/variable was asked for, where it was asked for and why. As it relates to the
'why', the Index used three symbols, an asterisk *, an obelisk †, and a double
obelisk ‡. According to Orton & Dieth (1962), an asterisk indicated "... phonological, an obelisk morphological, and a double obelisk syntactical significance" Orton & Dieth (1962: 47). "Key-word" items that bore none of the above-mentioned
marks meant that they were of lexical significance only. Part (B): Basic Material

consists of four volumes in three parts each. These four volumes – the *Six North-ern Localities and Man,* the *West Midland Counties,* the *East Midland Counties and East Anglia* and the *Southern Counties* – contained the variant responses to the questions asked during the survey. All responses were given in the then con-temporary, 1951 version of the IPA. These books therefore provided access to the several lexical and phonetic variants of a given item in the index of "Key-words". Part (D): The Linguistic Atlas presented a visual representation of the geographic distributions of the "Key-word" items and their lexical and phonetic variants (see §3.3.1).

3.2.3 The historical data

The principal source of English migrants to the British colonies, before 1776, con-sisted of indentured servants (Esposito et al. 1982). This large body of migrants included:

1. political prisoners, i.e. deported Royalists of the King's army. Between 1645 and 1650 the English Civil War contributed at least 8,000 indentured ser-vants to the West Indian colonies. This increase in the numbers of servants ran concurrent with the sugar boom that was being experienced in the 1640s and 1650s (Brewer & Susan 1996);

2. despairing English countrymen searching for a better life far from a so-cially and economically unstable England.

Determining the origin of these indentured servants involved scrutiny of a number of historical documents. The main body of historical data was taken from *The Complete Book of Emigrants: 1607–1660* (Coldham 1992; 1987), *The Bristol Reg-isters of Servants Sent to Foreign Plantations, 1654–1686* (Coldham 1988), and the *Virtual Jamestown, Virginia Center for Digital History* (VCDH) and the *British His-tory Online* databases (BHO), respectively. The second of the latter two sources afforded me access to documents such as the *Calendar of State Papers Colonial, America and the West Indies.* The *Calendar of State Papers,* which can be found in the British National Archives, is a set of some 1,000 historical papers concern-ing 16th to 18th century English activities in the American, Canadian, and West Indian colonies.

The Complete Book of Emigrants: 1607–1660 "... was conceived as an attempt to bring together from as many English sources ... a comprehensive account of emigration to the New World from its beginnings to 1660 ..." (Coldham 1987: vii). The book's content was compiled solely from English historical records and not

Irish, Welsh, Scottish or American sources (Coldham 1992; 1987). One of Cold-ham's (1992; 1987) sources included the *Colonial State Papers*; other sources in-cluded the *Port Books of London* (LVA), which provided information concerning indentured servant migration from London, to its American colonies within the period 1607–1660 (Coldham 1992; 1987).

The Bristol Register of Servants sent to Foreign Plantations, originally referred to as the *'Tolzey Book of Indentures'*, contained the systematic records of the in-dentures of over 10,000 English migrants. These were migrants who left from the port of Bristol, between 1654 and 1686, when the trade in indentured servants had reached its peak (Smith & IEAHC 1947; Morgan 1993). The original Tolzey Book or *Council Book*, which was entitled *Servants to Foreign Plantations*, consisted of two leather-bound volumes that can be found in the archives of the Corporation of the City of Bristol in England. In 1988 Peter Wilson Coldham compiled the set of records found in this two-part volume document, and made them accessible via the book, *The Bristol Registers of Servants Sent to Foreign Plantations, 1654–1686* (Coldham 1988).

In this book, i.e. *The Bristol Registers of Servants Sent to Foreign Plantations, 1654–1686*, Coldham (1988), as he did in *The Complete Book of Emigrants: 1607–1660* (Coldham 1992; 1987), provided information about indentured servants' names, dates of departure, destinations and the localities across England and the Isle of Man from which they were migrating between the years 1654 and 1686 (Sacks 1993). It is from this source that the *Virtual Jamestown, Virginia Center for Digi-tal History* (VCDH), created the online electronic registers database, which along-side Coldham's (1992; 1987) original work, was heavily consulted in carrying out this research.

British History Online is an online "digital library containing ... the core printed primary and secondary sources for the medieval and modern history of the British Isles... [It was] ... created by the Institute of Historical Research and the History of Parliament Trust and is ran by the Institute of Historical Research – the centre for the study of history in the United Kingdom – at the University of London" (BHO). This digital online library resource lived up to the aims of the Institute by having afforded me access to "... highly accurate digital versions of the core works of British history..." (BHO) such as the 17th century, *Calendar of State Pa-pers, Colonial America and West Indies* documents. The data from these state pa-pers, and the data collected from the above-discussed sources did their part in providing relevant answers to three questions that were asked of the historical sources. These questions were as follows:

1. Can we establish a chain of migration from England to Suriname, between

the years 1650 and 1667? Within these years Suriname was settled by the English and subsequently lost to the Dutch. After 1667 English migration to Suriname had ceased (see discussion in Chapter 6).

2. Can we establish a chain of migration from England, within the same time span mentioned in (1.), to the English colonies in the Caribbean and subsequently Suriname?

3. If the answer to (1.) and/or (2.) is in the affirmative, then what proportion of the total number of migrants to the Caribbean, including Suriname, is from the various localities across England?

3.2.4 Limitations

This study, as is the case with any type of research, suffers from a number of shortcomings. One shortcoming is that because of the time of the SED, i.e. 1950 to 1961, there is a circa 300 year gap between when this survey was done and when the first emigrants to Suriname left England. Nevertheless, the SED is held, to date, as the most detailed of its kind and the methodology employed by Orton et al. (1962–71) is still used as a standard when conducting similar types of surveys. This is echoed in the work of scholars as those who state that "... no reliable statements can be made about the widespread distribution of linguistic features within England without reference to its [the SED] findings..." (Kortmann & Schneider 2004: 29). Another shortcoming is that the Sranan data itself might not necessarily be completely characteristic of what 17th century "Sranan" would have sounded like; this is because no linguistic data source for 17th century Sranan was found and only data for 18th century Sranan were identified. Nevertheless, an attempt was made to find only the most archaic forms of Sranan, from the oldest Sranan data sources available. As listed in §3.2.1 above, two of these old data sources include the wordlists of Herlein (1718) and Schumann (1783).

Schumann's *Neger-Englisches WörterBuch*, which is a small dictionary, "... is one of the oldest and certainly one of the best..." sources of data for early Sranan (Arends 1989: 1). This assertion was also made by Kramp (1983), and Bruyn (1995) who held that Schumann's (1783) dictionary is a must have for any serious researcher of early Sranan. Schumann's (1783) work was integral in carrying out my research. This is because his dictionary afforded me access to two varieties of early Sranan; there are *Bakkratongo* ('White man's tongue') and 'the variety of the Blacks', i.e. *Ningretakki* (Schumann 1783). Herlein's (1718) work is a small collection of words and phrases that was created for travellers to Suriname. According to (Arends et al. 1995) Herlein's Sranan was *Bakkratongo*; i.e. 'the variety of the Whites'.

One other shortcoming of this study is that since I am neither a statistician nor historian, the strength of this research is to be found within the linguistic argumentation. Nevertheless, software such as R (see §3.4.3), and various scholars, from within the areas of Statistics and Dialect Geography were consulted along the way. As for the historical component of analysis, only the most authoritative sources, concerning 17th century England and her colonies, were utilised in this research (see §3.2.3). Also, having undertaken three independent types of analysis, i.e. statistics, linguistic feature mapping and historical analysis of migration patterns from England, and arriving at comparable results, this was taken as strong evidence that the research findings are sound.

3.3 Data compilation, tagging and database creation

3.3.1 Data compilation

The following steps were taken in collecting the data from the sources discussed in §3.2:

1. The dictionary and wordlists of Sranan Tongo were checked for all words of potential Anglo-Saxon origin. To identify these words and their linguistic origins the following sources were consulted: the etymological information in Wilner's (2007; 2003; 1992) *Dictionary of Sranan Tongo*, the Sranan wordlists of Stichting Volkslectuur (Stichting 1980), Schumann (1783), Von Fermin (1769), and Herlein (1718) and Smith's (2008a, 1987) historical phonology works. In addition, words similar in form and meaning across Sranan and English were checked with dictionaries of the other European languages known to have influenced Sranan, notably Portuguese and Dutch. These dictionaries included: Vieyra (1860) *A Dictionary of the English and Portuguese Languages* and Stevenson (1823) 's *English and Dutch Dictionary*. Since my research dealt only with words of Anglo-Saxon origin, these dictionaries helped in the sifting out of items that could possibly have originated in any of the other languages mentioned above.

2. The result of step (1.) was a wordlist of 529 words. This wordlist was used to check against Orton's Index of Key-Words (Orton & Dieth 1962) and their regional, lexical and phonetic variant forms, which were the subject of the SED survey.

3. Where no match was found, a check was made of the Key-Word headings in the actual SED Responses Books (Orton et al. 1962–71) for any variants that might match the remaining items not found as a result of step (2.). This was an important stage since dialectal realisations of a given etymon were not always presented in Orton's Index of Key-Words. Carrying out this step ensured that all possible input forms were accounted for. The remaining items, for which no SED entries could be found, were removed from the wordlist.

4. The result of the application of steps (2.) and (3.) was a reduced list of 497 potential SED word etyma. Those words that I found to be invariant across the English dialects surveyed in the SED were also removed from this reduced list. Consequently, the list of 497 potential input etyma decreased to a list of 45 SED items. These items were then taken as the 45 SED word variables, hereafter referred to as the SED45, that were used in this study. These were as follows:

Table 3.1: The 45 SED Word variables

1. *arse*	13. *finger*	25. *horse*	37. *remember*
2. *ask*	14. *fire*	26. *hot*	38. *star*
3. *broth*	15. *first*	27. *house*	39. *teeth*
4. *brother*	16. *four*	28. *hungry*	40. *turn*
5. *burn*	17. *gold*	29. *hurt*	41. *wear*
6. *care*	18. *gutter*	30. *iron*	42. *work* (noun)
7. *cold*	19. *hand*	31. *master* (hus.)	43. *work* (verb)
8. *corn*	20. *hare*	32. *more* (quant.)	44. *woman*
9. *curse*	21. *head*	33. *more* (comp.)	45. *yesterday*
10. *door*	22. *hear*	34. *mouth*	
11. *ear*	23. *help*	35. *old*	
12. *eye*	24. *herring*	36. *pig* (hog)	

KEY		
hus. husband	**comp.** comparative	**quant.** quantity

5. The SED45 word variables were then scrutinised and tagged based on the linguistic feature or group of linguistic features that they exhibited. This process of identification and labelling of the linguistic features that I no-

ticed across the SED45 word variables was not a difficult task. This is because these features represented a subset of the same linguistic features that received a great deal of attention by Orton et al. (1962–71) for their regional specificity. In the works of other dialect geographers such as Wells (1982), some of these features, for example rhoticity, were presented as salient features that partition England into various dialect regions. Wells (1982) stated for example, that "... the preservation of ... /r/ in all environments is the best-known phonetic characteristic of the west of England" (p. 341). There were eight of these linguistic features in total and it is important to note that in a few cases some of the SED45 word variables had more than one of these eight features.

3.3.2 Tagging the data: The linguistic features

The SED45 word variables, as mentioned above, exhibited one or a combination of more than one of eight linguistic features. These linguistic features, which consist of one variable lexical feature and seven variable phonetic features, are presented in Table 3.2.

Table 3.2: The linguistic features and their corresponding tags

Linguistic Features	Feature Tags
Lexical Variant feature	**±LexVar**
Post-vocalic /r/	**±PVR**
Word-initial phonemic ⟨h⟩ feature	**±h**
Dental Fricative feature	**±DF**
Labial Voicing feature	**±LVoc**
Word-initial Palatal feature	**±Pal**
Consonant Cluster Reversal feature	**±CCR**
Diphthong feature	**±Diph**
KEY	
± Feature is present or absent	

The ±LexVar tag was used to label SED45 variables with more than one word variant. One example was the variable *pig* which in the SED exhibited +LexVar *pig* and *hog*. The Sranan reflex is [hagu], which therefore indicated to me that the input had to be from a *hog* dialect and not a *pig* dialect (see §3.3.2.1 for discussion of this feature).

33

The ±PVR tag was used to label SED45 variables whose variants were either rhotic or not. Take the example of variables *care* and *turn*. Their Sranan reflexes, [ke] and [trʌn], indicated that the SED input variant of these two variables had to be –PVR and +PVR, respectively (see §3.3.2.2 for discussion of this feature).

The ±h tag was used to label variables whose variants exhibited one of three variant realisations of /h/ in word-initial positions, or no realisation of this phoneme at all. This was noticed, for example, with the variables *hear, hare* and *woman*. Their Sranan realisations, [jerɪ], [he] and [wʊma/hʊman] respectively, indicated that SED variants for these reflexes had to be /h/-full (see §3.3.2.3 for discussion).

The ±DF tag was used to label word variables whose variants displayed variation between /θ/~/t/~/f/, and variation between /ð/~/d/~/v/ in syllable-final and word-medial positions, respectively. This was seen with variables *mouth* and *brother* for example. The Sranan reflexes were [mofo] and [brada], which indicated to me that the SED input variants had to be –DF. Although the input for these items would need to be –DF, the input was also not +[t] and +[v], respectively. To the contrary, the input for *mouth* had to be an etymon with syllable-final /f/ and the etyma for *brother* had to be an etymon with word-medial /d/. Of course, the possibility exists, that the voiced and voiceless dental fricatives could themself have undergone, in the colonies, alterations to /d/ and /f/ respectively (see §3.3.2.4 for further discussion).

The ±LVoc tag was used to label word variables whose variants displayed variation between /f/ and its voiced counterpart /v/, in word initial positions. This feature was observed with the variable *four*, for example. The Sranan reflex, [fɔ], indicated that the input form had to be –LVoc since no instances of [fɔ] were identified across the Sranan data (see §3.3.2.5 for discussion).

The ±Pal tag was used to label variables whose variants exhibited variation between the phonetic realisation and non-realisation of /j/ in word initial positions. One variable that exhibited this feature was *yesterday*. The Sranan reflex [esrede] indicated to me that either the /j/ was deleted in Sranan or it was not realised in the input itself. The SED data did, however, show /j/~ ∅ variation with this word and so I therefore took this to mean that the input form must have been –Pal (see §3.3.2.7 for discussion).

The ±CCR tag was used to label word variables whose variants displayed variation between word-final consonantal sequences [_ks] and [_sk]. The item *ask* was the only word variable for which this was relevant and its Sranan reflex [hak-isi] indicated that the [_ks] sequence was preferred. This meant that the input form had to be +CCR (see §3.3.2.8 for discussion).

The ±Diph tag was used to label word variables whose variants had either a monophthong or diphthong in the same phonetic environment, i.e. preceding the lateral approximant [l] in [(C)_l(C)] constructions. The consonants indicated in brackets are optional. For example, the Sranan reflex for the variable *cold* [kowru] indicated that the input had to be +Diph. A note had to be made about the realisation of the /l/ in Sranan, even though it was not a feature under study. Across the data where there was an expectation to see /l/, /r/ was noticed. This same phenomenon was noticed while investigating Sranan on the two fieldtrips mentioned in Chapter 1; at that time it was hypothesized that Sranan did not distinguish between the two sounds. A later reading of Smith's (2004) work on the phonology of the Surinamese creoles provided an explanation of the phenomenon. In this work, they stated that there was a tendency for Suriname creoles "... to neutralize the distinction between /l/ and /r/... [and in the case of Sranan, this process was incomplete because]... word-internal liquids go to [r] ... [but word-initial liquids go] to [l] ..." (Smith & Haabo 2004: 562). The eight feature tags and the SED45 items that display these tags are discussed in more detail in §3.3.2.1 to §3.3.2.8 on the following pages.

3.3.2.1 Lexical variant feature (±LexVar)

The ±LexVar tag was used to label SED45 word variables that exhibited more than one lexical variant; the ±LexVar tag therefore meant [+lexical] variant, i.e. the SED45 word variable had a lexical variant, or [−lexical] variant, which meant the logical opposite. These SED45 word variants in some cases distinguished speakers of one dialect from speakers of another dialect and these variants therefore helped to narrow the search for potential dialect sources for Sranan. The SED45 word variables that exhibited this feature are presented in Table 3.3.

The Sranan reflexes presented in the third column of Table 3.3, highlight the fact that the relevant SED45 etyma for [ras], [hagu], [masra], [memere], [gotro], [he], [jesi], [hedi], [tifi], [brafu] and [mofo] must have been, *arse, pig, master* (husband), *remember, gutter, hare, ears, head, teeth, broth* and *mouth*, respectively and no other dialectal variants. Table 3.3 also highlights the fact that the SED45 input must have exhibited certain phonetic features, for them to be considered the precise input forms for the Sranan reflexes, hereafter referred to as the Sranan45. The distributions of these features were as follows:

- [he] *hare*, with +h and −PVR,

- [ras] *arse*, [memere] *remember*, [masra] *master* (husband) and [gotro] *gutter* with +PVR,

Table 3.3: SED Variables with the ±LexVar feature and their Sranan reflexes

Words Variables	Lexical Variants	Sranan Reflex
arse	arse, bottom	[ras]
broth	soaks, broth	[brafu]
ears	lugs, ears	[jesi]
gutter	(water)-sprout, gutter	[gotro]
hare	(old) sall, hare	[he]
head	napper, head	[hedi]
master (husband)	master, (old) man, husband	[masra]
mouth	gob, mouth	[mofo]
pig	hog, pig	[hagu]
remember	mind, remember	[memere]
teeth	tushies, teeth	[tifi]

- [brafu] *broth*, [mofo] *mouth* and [tifi] *teeth* with −DF,

- [hedi] *head* and [hagu] *pig*, with +h,

- [jesi] *ears*, with +Pal and −PVR.

3.3.2.2 The post-vocalic /r/ feature (±PVR)

One of the major phonetic divides in England is rhoticity, which is a feature that readily splits England into /r/-full and /r/-less dialect areas. This was a phenomenon noticed by Wells (1982). This linguistic feature involves phonetic realisations of ⟨r⟩ after a vowel sound (Roca & Johnson 1999). This was noticed, for example, with the SED45 word variable *hare*, with +PVR variants [ɛər], [ɛːr], [heːəɾ] respectively, produced in localities Saxby (Lincolnshire), Hanmer (Cheshire) and Himely (Staffordshire) (Orton & Barry 1970). In non-rhotic accents, on the other hand, the ⟨r⟩ is never phonetically realized after vowel sounds. Non-rhotic SED45 *hare* variants that were noticed across the SED data included [hɛə], [ɛːr], [eə], produced in localities such as Great Snoring (Norfolk), Little Harrowden (Northamptonshire) and Great Chesterford (Essex), respectively (Orton & Tilling 1970).

The Sranan data showed evidence of both rhotic and non-rhotic English input. This influence was exhibited in Sranan reflexes such as [ke] *care* and [he] *hare* that are −PVR, and [moro] *more* and [jeri] *hear*, which are +PVR. Smith (1987: 30) dealt with this phenomenon by stating that "... the English element in Sranan consists of a mixture of r-less and r-full dialects," with some words coming from rhotic dialects and others coming from non-rhotic ones.

Alternatively, I hypothesise that Sranan might have been influenced by a single dialect or cluster of geo-linguistically related dialects, which exhibited ±PVR on specific words. The latter hypothesis could only be taken as fact, if and only if a single locality or group of localities in close geographic proximity provided the specific ±PVR SED45 input variants for the Sranan45 reflexes (see Chapter 5). The SED45 word variables for which this phonetic feature was relevant are presented in Table 3.4.

Table 3.4: SED variables with the ±PVR feature and their Sranan reflexes

Words Variables	Sranan Reflex
burn	[bron]
care	[ke]
corn	[karu]
curse	[kosi]
door	[doro]
iron	[aje]
more (comparative)	[moro]
more (quantifier)	[moro]
star	[stari]
turn	[tron]
wear	[weri]

Across the SED45 the actual pronunciation of phonemic postvocalic ⟨r⟩ varied. Take for example the word variable *wear*, which in the data exhibited variants with the alveolar central approximant, the alveolar trill and the retroflex tap/flap; i.e. [wɛəɹ], [wɪər] and [wɛəɽ] produced in Harmondsworth (Middlesex), Long-town (Cumberland) and East Harting (Sussex), respectively. There was also the presence of variants that exhibited r-colouring, which Wells (1982) considered to be a type of rhoticity which is marked on vowels, i.e. the vowel is produced with /r/-like qualities. Wells (1982) indicated that this phenomenon was indicative of the west of England, where the "preservation of historical /r/ in all environments is best known" (p. 342). An example of this kind of rhoticity was seen with *wear* [wɛɹ], produced in Blagdon (Somersetshire). In this work, all word/syllable-final consonantal realisations of ⟨r⟩, along with r-colouring, were taken as +PVR and the absence of any consonantal realisation of this variable as –PVR.

3.3.2.3 Word-initial phonemic /h/ feature ±h

Phonemic /h/, like rhoticity, is considered to be a very salient feature in English dialect geography. The realisation, or lack thereof, of some consonantal form of /h/ in syllable-initial positions, is a feature that is diagnostic of English dialectal regions and social stratification within England. According to Beal (2004), "pronunciation of initial ⟨h⟩ is socially stratified in most areas of the North as in most of England" (p. 12). Trudgill (2004: 174), for example, highlighted the fact that with the exception of Norwich and Ipswich, "… Traditional Dialects in East Anglia do not have h-dropping." This is in contrast to the "… vernacular accents of the Midland and Midland North [of England]…" for example, where Clark (2004: 157) found /h/-dropping in initial positions to be a prevalent feature. The SED45 word variables that shared this single phonetic feature are presented in Table 3.5.

Table 3.5: SED variables with the ±h feature and their Sranan reflexes

Words Variables	Sranan Reflex
ask	[hakisi]
eye	[hai]
hand	[han]
head	[hedi]
help	[helpi]
herring	[heren]
hot	[hati]
house	[hoso]
hungry	[hangri]
woman	[human/wuman]

The SED45 word variables with the ±h exhibited three variant realisations. Phonemic /h/ occurred as (1) the palatal approximant [j], before mid to high front vowels or as the labio-velar approximant [w] before back vowels; (2) it occurred as the voiceless glottal fricative [h] in both pre-vocalic environments mentioned in (1); or (3) this pre-vocalic consonant was dropped completely. This was seen for example with [jɛɽɪn], [hɛɽɪn], [ɛɽən], the SED45 variants for *herring*, as produced in Wedmore (Somersetshire), Latterbridge (Gloucestershire) and Altarnun

(Cornwall), respectively. This distribution of sED45 word variants suggests that the feature should be treated as ternary. However, this feature is also binary since the variants of the /h/, as mentioned above, are phonologically conditioned. sED45 word variables which exhibited this ±h feature were therefore taken as either [+consonant], in which case variants occurred with one of the phonetically conditioned realisations of /h/, or [−consonant], in which case I did not observe any consonantal realisations of /h/. In light of this, I took the following approach in dealing with this feature:

- treat all sED45 variants with /h/ →[h], as /h/-full;

- treat all sED45 reflexes with /h/→[j] or [w], as /h/-full;

- treat all sED45 reflexes with /h/→∅ , as /h/-less.

The Sranan45 reflexes presented in Table 3.5 were therefore all treated as being /h/-full. This meant that their sED45 input variants must also have been /h/-full.

3.3.2.4 Dental fricative/labial feature (±DF)

The ±DF feature, allowed for a distinction to be made between dialects that produced sED45 items *teeth*, *broth* and *mouth*, with: (1) the voiceless labiodental fricative [f], in word-final position, for example [tiːf], [bɾɔːf] and [mæʊf], produced in Brompton Regis, Wedmore and Blagdon (all in Somersetshire), respectively; (2) the voiceless dental fricative [θ], in word final positions, as seen with [tiːθ], [brɒθ] and [mʌʊθ], produced in Melonsby (Yorkshire); (3) the voiceless dental/alveolar plosive [t], as seen with [brɒt], produced in York (Yorkshire); and (4) those areas which exhibited a combination of (2) and (3).

sED45 word variables that exhibited this linguistic feature also showed dialectal variation between areas that produced the item *brother* with: (1) the intervocalic labiodental fricative [v], as seen with [brʌvə] produced in Hackney (Middlesex); (2) the inter-vocalic dental fricative [ð], as seen with [broðə], produced in Marshside (Lancashire); (3) the alveolar plosive [d], as seen with [brʊdə], produced in Yealand (Lancashire); and (4) those areas which exhibited a combination of (2) and (3). In the Sranan45 data, no voiced labio-dental or voiced inter-dental fricative variants were observed for this item. The word variable *brother* is also diagnostic of PVR (see §3.3.2.7). The Sranan reflexes of *teeth*, *broth* and *mouth* are presented in Table 3.6.

Table 3.6: SED variables with the ±DF feature and their Sranan reflexes

Words Variables	Sranan Reflex
broth	[brafu]
brother	[brada]
mouth	[mofo]
teeth	[tifi]

In the Sranan45 data, neither the voiceless and voiced dental fricatives, i.e. [θ] and [ð] respectively, nor the voiced alveolar fricative [v], was observed. In fact English /v/, as seen with Sranan items [èbi] *heavy*, [lobi] *love* and [ibri] *every*, is realised as the voiced bilabial plosive [b], in all cases (Smith 1987; Smith & Haabo 2004) and /ð/ is realised as [d], also in all cases, as is evident from [brada] *brother* in Table 3.6 (Smith 1987; Smith & Haabo 2004). In syllable-initial positions, [t] was observed, as seen with Sranan's [tangi] *thanks*. In syllable-final positions, [f] was observed, as seen from Table 3.6. Smith (1987); Smith & Haabo (2004) noticed the same pattern with [t] and [θ]. He explained, that while "other creole languages generally replaced /θ/ by /t/ in all positions with only occasional examples of /f/ ... [it is quite possible that] ... [θ] did not appear very frequently ... in the English that provided the model for Proto-Sranan ..." (Smith 1987: 244). Smith (1987) was very careful in how he worded this statement; he neither confirmed nor denied the possible influence of the dental fricative in Proto-Sranan.

It was evident to me, based on the data in Table 3.6, that the SED45 input etyma must have been with word-final [f] and not [t]. Since it was obvious that the influence was not from a /t/ dialect, I tried to determine whether in the case of Sranan, the [f] influence was derived from a /ð/ dialect, or from a /f/ dialect, but this was to no avail. However, as was mentioned in the previous paragraph, other creoles have been found to interchange pronunciation of [ð] for [f] within the same phonetic environment, i.e. in word-final positions. This meant that it was possible that /ð/ could have also become [f] in Sranan and/or that [f]~[ð] and [ð] migrants to Suriname may have involuntarily opted to "level-out" this word-final phonetic feature variation to [f], over some period of time. I therefore took as the putative input for *teeth*, *broth* and *mouth*, all SED45 word variants with syllable-final [ð], [f] or [ð]~[f].

3.3.2.5 The diphthong feature (±Diph)

The sed45 word variables that exhibited only one linguistic feature were *cold, old* and *gold*. In the sed, their variants show divisions between dialect areas that had monophthongs in these items, for example [kɔːld], [ɔːld] and [gɔːld] produced in Patterdale (Westmorland), Abbeytown (Cumberland) and Witton-le-Wear (Durham), respectively; and those that produced them with a diphthong in the same inter-consonantal environments. This was seen, for example, with [kɔʊld], [ɒʊld] and [gɔʊld] produced in Farningham (Kent), Skenfrith (Monmouthshire) and Eningale (Staffordshire), respectively. The sed45 reflexes for these words are presented in Table 3.7.

Table 3.7: sed Variables with the ±Diph feature and their Sranan reflexes

Words Variables	Sranan Reflex
cold	[kouru]
gold	[goutu]
old	[ouru]

The Sranan reflexes presented in Table 3.7 suggested a diphthongal as opposed to a monophthongal English input, for these items. Since this was the case, I only took as potential sed45 inputs, variants with diphthongal realisations for *cold gold* and *old*; these include, for example [kæʊld], [æʊld] and [goʊld] produced in Deerhurst (Gloucestershire), Checkley (Herefordshire) and Romsley (Worcestershire) respectively. The three remaining phonetic features, i.e. the labial voicing feature (±LVoc), the word-initial palatal feature (±Pal) and the consonant cluster reversal feature (±CCR), were not observed in isolation. These three features occurred with word variables that also exhibited the ±LexVar, ±PVR, ±h, etc. These combinations, along with the others that were identified, are presented in Table 3.8 on page 42.

3.3.2.6 The lexical variant feature and other feature(s)

Eleven sed45 word variables had the ±LexVar plus one or two other features. These variables, as indicated in Table 3.7, were: *arse, broth, ears, hare, head, hog, gutter, master, mouth, remember,* and *teeth.* The Sranan realisations of these variables are [ras], [brafu], [jesi], [he], [hedi], [hog], [gotro], [masra], [memere] and

Table 3.8: SED Variables with Combinations of two or more Features

Variables	±LexVar	±PVR	±h	±DF	±LVoc	±Pal	±CCR
arse	1	1	–	–	–	–	–
ears	1	0	–	–	–	–	–
gutter	1	1	–	–	–	–	–
master	1	1	–	–	–	–	–
remember	1	1	–	–	–	–	–
hare	1	0	1	–	–	–	–
head	1	–	1	–	–	–	–
hog	1	–	1	–	–	–	–
broth	1	–	–	1	–	–	–
mouth	1	–	–	0	–	–	–
teeth	1	–	–	0	–	–	–
hear	–	1	1	–	–	–	–
hungry	–	1	1	–	–	–	–
brother	–	0	–	0	–	–	–
finger	–	0	–	–	0	–	–
fire	–	0	–	–	0	–	–
first	–	0	–	–	0	–	–
four	–	0	–	–	0	–	–
yesterday	–	0	–	–	0	–	–
ask	–	–	1	–	–	–	1

KEY

±LexVar and other features	1	Feature articulated
±PVR and other features	0	Feature not articulated
±h and other features		

[tifi], respectively. I have already discussed, in §3.3.2.1, what this meant for the SED input; this is restated below. The input needed to be one that had:

- *hare* with +h and −PVR;

- *arse, remember, master* (husband) and *gutter* with +PVR;

- *broth, mouth* and *teeth* with −DF;

- *head* and *hog* (pig) with +h;

- *ears*, with +Pal;

3.3.2.7 The rhoticity feature and other feature

Eight word variables exhibited a combination of the ±PVR feature and one other feature. These variables are, *brother, finger, fire, first, four, hear, hungry* and *yesterday*. The Sranan reflexes for these variables are [brada], [faija], [fɪŋga], [fosi], [fɔ], [jeri], [haŋgri] and [esrede], respectively. The SED input variants therefore needed to be:

- *brother* with −DF and −PVR;

- *finger, fire, first*, and *four* with −LVoc and −PVR;

- *hear*, and *hungry* with +h and −PVR;

- *yesterday* with −Pal and +PVR;

3.3.2.8 The word-initial phonemic /h/ feature and other feature

The remaining word variable that exhibited a combination of features was *ask*. This variable is realised as [hakisi] in Sranan, which meant that its SED input variant had to be one that exhibited the features +h and +CCR.

At first, the assumption was made that the word-initial /h/ could have been a case of hypercorrection. However, as I scrutinised the SED data, it became very evident that /h/-full variants of this variable could be found across England. As it relates to the CCR feature, my first assumption was that the [_ks] feature was a Sranan feature that was not attributable to England. However, the data proved otherwise by providing evidence of the existence of this phenomenon across England.

There is one matter left to address, concerning the data discussed so far. This involves the phonological conversion rules which account for the lexico-phonetic shapes of the 45 Sranan reflexes. These are discussed in §3.3.2.9 below. After the presentation of these conversion rules, I then move on to a discussion of the research design.

3.3.2.9 Phonological conversion rules

The presentation of the conversion processes that account for the phonetic shapes of the Sranan45 reflexes, were taken from a number of sources. These include the works of Smith (1977; 1987; 2008a), DeCamp & Hancock (1974), Holm (1988), and Plag & Uffmann (2000). These conversion processes, as expressed across the above-mentioned sources, took place as a result of the phonotactic constraints of the West African language(s) of enslaved Africans, which stipulated open CV (consonant followed by vowel) syllable structures as opposed to complex ones. These conversion processes included insertion of a paragogic vowel, epenthesis, metathesis and deletion; I begin the discussion by looking at vowel paragoge, one of the major features noticed across the majority of the Sranan45 items.

Vowel paragoge is the process by which non-etymological vowel sounds are added to words ending in a consonant sound (Plag & Uffmann 2000). There is some contention over whether there was one default paragogic vowel in Sranan (see Smith 1977), which would, depending on the vowel in the English word, change to either [a] as seen with [masra], [e] as seen with [memere], and [o] as seen with [moro] for example (see Plag & Uffmann 2000). I do not enter into a discussion of this issue here, except to say that there are five observable paragogic vowels in Sranan; these vowels are [i], [e], [a], [o] and [u] (see Plag & Uffmann 2000: 311). Since I am not concerned with determining which vowel was the default paragogic vowel I relaxed Smith's (1977) proposed rule for the insertion of the word-final paragogic vowel to:

$$\emptyset \rightarrow [V(i, e, a, o, u)] \ / \ VC\$$$

The rule above states that where an English word, whose syllable(s) did not end with a final nasal consonant, as with [bron], *burn* and [tron] *turn* for example, was introduced to the enslaved Africans, one of five paragogic vowels was added; this is seen, for instance, with [hedi] *head*. This rule accounts for the majority of the Sranan45 forms. However, it does not fully account for the following items: [memere] *remember*, [goutu] *gold*, [gotro] *gutter*, [masra] *master*, [karu] *corn*, [bron] *burn*, [ouru] *old*, [kouru] *cold*, [tron] *turn*, [wroko] *work* (verb), [wroko] *work* (noun), [ras] *arse*, and [heren] *herring*.

With the words, [bron] *burn*, [tron] *turn*, [wroko] *work* (verb), [wroko] *work* (noun), and [ras] *arse* the process of metathesis was at play.

What occurred was a swapping of the positions of the liquid and the preceding vowel as expressed by the following rule:

CVLC →CLVC (*see DeCamp & Hancock 1974)

What this expresses is the fact that in the production of a word such as *work* the liquid was no longer articulated after the vowel [o] but immediately after [w] and before the [o], thereby resulting in [wroko]. According to Holm (1988), this feature of Sranan might actually have been the result of two historical conversion processes. In his rendition, the enslaved Africans, after inserting an epenthetic vowel to break up consonant clusters such as found in *work*, shifted the stress in the new word and then, via a process of elision, deleted the original vowel sound. Holm's (1988) conversion process can be expressed as follows:

1. ∅ →[V] / [CV́C_C]   (epenthesis)
2. [CV́cvc] →[cvcV́C]   (stress shift)
3. V→∅ / [C_cvc]   (deletion of original vowel)

For the remainder of the words, consonant clusters were reduced via deletion of a segment, as seen with [t] in [masra] *master*. The following section is a discussion of the research design and how the data discussed above were processed and used in carrying out this research.

3.4 Research design

This research attempted to answer the three questions presented in Chapter 1, using the data discussed in the preceding sections. Restated below, these questions are:

1. What do lexico-phonetic correspondences between Sranan words and their English dialectal etyma tell us about where within England this influence might have originated?

2. What can (1.) above tell us about the competing hypotheses concerning the source of lexico-phonetic input in Sranan, i.e. a pan-dialectal account versus a mono-dialectal account?

3. What kind of corroboration for or challenge to the proposed dialect area(s) do we find in the historical records?

In attempting to answer these questions a method of triangulation was employed, via the combination of three independent types of analysis, i.e. statistical linguistics, dialect geography and the 17th century history of English. Triangulation broadly defined, is the "combination of methodologies in the study of the same phenomenon ... [It is a method aimed at capturing] ... a more complete, holistic and contextual portrayal of the unit under study ... [and in so doing it offers a more enriched] ... understanding, by allowing for new or deeper dimensions to emerge ..." (Denzin 1978: 603–604). In essence, triangulation allows for greater accuracy of results, since a given topic is assessed from more than one independent viewpoint. Hereafter is a presentation of how the data discussed above were used and assessed using this proposed three-part methodological tool.

3.4.1 Database creation

Two Microsoft Excel databases were constructed using the tagged data discussed in the preceding sections. The first one was the SED45 database. This database was made up of all SED lexical and phonetic variants for each of the 45 word variables discussed thus far. The second database, the Sranan45 database, was made up of the specific Sranan realisations, i.e. the putative input forms for each of the 45 SED diagnostic word variables found in the SED45 database. Both Excel databases were saved in .csv (comma-separated variables) format.

3.4.1.1 The SED45 database

Each SED word variable and its lexical and/or phonetic variants was presented in relation to the 313 localities surveyed in the SED (see §3.2.2). The organization of this database was as follows:

1. All 313 localities were placed in Column 1, in vertical order from numbers 1 to 313. In accordance with Orton et al. (1962–71), these numbers represented all the localities from the north and the Isle of Man, to the west, to the east and to the south, in that order, across England. 1 to 75 represented the localities in the north of England and the Isle of Man, 76 to 151 represented the localities in the west, 152 to 238 represented the localities in the east and 239 to 313 represented the localities in the south of England, respectively (see Appendix).

2. Each SED45 word variable along with its relevant feature tag(s), was presented, a word-per-column in the first row of the series of columns to the right of the first column, i.e. in the first row of columns 2 to 46 following the locality column (see Table 3.9).

3. Within each cell of the word variable columns, i.e. columns 2 to 46, a binary coding system was used to indicate whether a word variant was produced with or without one or a combination of more than one, of the eight linguistic features. The symbol 1 was used to indicate the realisation of a word variant with the presence of the indicated linguistic feature/s. The symbol 0 was used to indicate the presence of a word variant with non-presence of the indicated linguistic feature/s, or the total absence of a word variant (see Chapter 4). This meant that each of the 313 rows represented an actually existing combination (EC) vector of variants for the 45 word variables. This is illustrated in Table 3.9.

Table 3.9: SED45 database (Sample)

Vectors	⟶			
↓SED Localities	*House*	*Hand*	*Hog*	*Hurt*
	±h	±h	±LexVar & ±h	±h & ±PVR
2	1	1	1	0
3	1	1	1	0
4	1	1	1	0
109	0	0	0	0

3.4.1.2 The Sranan45 Database

Each Sranan45 reflex of the SED45 word variables was itself placed in an Excel database, in the same order as found in the SED45 database, i.e. an item-per-column from left-to-right. A 0 was used to indicate the presence of a reflex that is characterised by the non-presence of the indicated linguistic feature/s, and a 1 was used to represent the presence of a reflex that is characterised by the manifestation of the indicated linguistic feature/s (see Table 3.10). The resulting horizontal, left to right vector of 0s and 1s represented what the putative 17th century English dialectal input would have needed to resemble.

3.4.2 Using the SED45 and the Sranan45 databases

The horizontal vector sequence (hereafter, vector) of all 45 reflexes in the Sranan45 database represented what a potential English input dialect needed to resemble for it to be taken as the input of origin. This Sranan45 vector of reflexes

Table 3.10: Sranan45 database (Sample)

Target Vector ⟶				
	House	*Hand*	*Hog*	*Hurt*
	±h	±h	±LexVar & ±h	±h & ±PVR
	1	1	1	1

was therefore used to search all 313 existing combinations of SED45 word variants exhibited by each of the 313 SED dialects in the SED45 database. The goal was to determine the extent to which any locality or group of localities in the SED45 database corresponded with the specific Sranan45 forms. An illustration of how the Sranan45 and the SED45 were used is presented in Table 3.11.

Table 3.11: Using the Sranan45 and SED45 databases

Target Vector ⟶				
Sranan	*House*	*Hand*	*Hog*	*Hurt*
	±h	±h	±LexVar & ±h	±h & ±PVR
	1	1	1	1
EC Vector ⟶				
SED Localities	*House*	*Hand*	*Hog*	*Hurt*
	±h	±h	±LexVar & ±h	±h & ±PVR
2	1	1	1	0
3	1	1	1	0
4	1	1	1	0
109	0	0	0	0

KEY			
	Variant non-match	**±LexVar**	Lexical variant present/absent
	Variant match		
2	Earsdon	**±h**	⟨h⟩ present/absent
3	Ellington		
4	Embleton	**±PVR**	post-vocalic ⟨r⟩ present/absent
109	Warslow		

The Sranan45 reflexes vector found in the Sranan Database (sample) in Table 3.11 is 1111, i.e. *house, hand* with +h, the presence of *hog* with +LexVar and +h and *hurt* with +h and −PVR. When we use this to check against the SED45 Database (sample), the following results are evident:

- localities 2, 3 and 4 with their 1110 vector, have a ¾ correspondence with the putative input;

- locality 109, with its 0000 vector, exhibits a ¼ correspondence.

What this process allowed for was three-fold. First, as seen with locality 109, it allowed for the sifting out of localities whose SED variants did not correspond to the Sranan45 reflexes. Second, it highlighted all SED localities that shared the same degree of correspondence. Third, it highlighted the varying degrees of correspondence between actually existing combinations (EC) of SED variants per locality vector and the Sranan45. The search was for one SED locality or geographically related localities whose actual existing combination of variants exhibited 100% correspondence with the Sranan45 reflexes vector. By successfully finding such a locality or group of localities, I could then hypothesise, with a high degree of certainty, that this locality or group of localities represented the area(s) of origin for the Sranan45 (see §3.4.3.2 for a discussion of partial matches). Such evidence would present major problems for a pan-dialectal account of origin, in which linguistic features are said to be selected "by-chance" from localities all over England.

3.4.3 Statistical analysis (Component 1 of the assessment tool)

The SED45 and the Sranan45 Excel databases were imported into the statistical analysis tool (Cran) R. It is with this programme that the process described in §3.4.2 was undertaken. This cutting edge open-source software is a computing "environment in which classical and modern statistical techniques have been implemented." What this software allows for, among other things, is a variety of linear and nonlinear modelling, statistical calculations, clustering analysis, etc. (R Core Team 2011).

Within this computing environment, the Sranan vector of 0s and 1s contained in the Sranan45 database, was used to check against each of the 313 vectors with their 45 variant combinations that were housed in the SED45 database. I did consider the possibility that given the times at which the various SED and Sranan data were collected (see §3.2), some internal linguistic change and or other extraneous factors might have been involved. This would mean that finding a full match was unlikely. Provisions therefore needed to be made to deal with partial matches and determining how statistically significant these would be in determining the origin of the English influence in Sranan (see §3.4.3.2).

3.4.3.1 Calculating probability of a mono-dialectal origin

The degree of correspondence between the 45 items, across the 313 dialects in the SED45 database, and their lexical and/or phonetic reflexes in the Sranan45 database, would be used to calculate what "by-chance" probability (see Chapter 4). What this meant was that there was a need to calculate the likelihood of finding a horizontal SED vector of English variants, with the specific combination of features discussed in §3.3, from across the 313 actual existing vectors of variants in the SED45 database.

The first step was to establish the total number of Possible Combinations (PC) of the variants for the SED45 word variables. This gave a sense of the number of combinations of SED word variants for the 45 SED word variables. In calculating the PCvalue, a binary system of calculation was used (see Chapter 4). To this end, the stance was taken that for any corpus containing 45 lexico-phonetic SED45 word variables two possibilities existed:

1. there is the specific combination of the eight linguistic features across the 45 items, in which case there is a "match" with the items in the Sranan45 database;

2. there is a different combination, in which case a "non-match" will occur.

In light of these two possibilities, the SED45 word variables therefore represented a vector of length 45 (variants), with each SED word variant being [±match] with a vector of reflexes in the Sranan45 database. Consequently, the number of possible distinct vectors was calculated as 2^{45}. This means that there were 35 trillion, 184 billion, 372 million, 88 thousand and 832 (35,184,372,088,832) possible distinct vectors, hereafter shortened to $3.52 * 10^{13}$.

The second step was to establish, via identification and counting, the number of actually Existing Combinations (EC) of sequences of variants for the 45 SED word variables across the 313 locality vectors in the SED45 database. This figure was taken as the 313 localities in the SED database. With the EC figure secured, the next step would be to then establish the probability (p), of a 100% EC vector and Sranan45 vector correspondence being a "by chance" occurrence. The approach to measuring the probability that a 100% correspondence between an EC vector and the Sranan45 vector happened "by-chance" was a concept borrowed from within the area of probability and statistics.

"Probability and statistics are concerned with events that happen by chance ..." (DeCoursey 2003: 1) and an example of a by chance event is that stated above. This involves identifying an EC vector, from across the 313 vectors in the SED45 database, which fully corresponds to the Sranan45 vector, given $3.52 * 10^{13}$ PC of distinct vectors. This is similar to the act of flipping a coin; the element of chance exists because "... we cannot predict with any certainty the outcome of a particular trial ..." (DeCoursey 2003: 1), or as it relates to the data, finding, as illustrated in §3.4.2 above, an actual 100% EC to Sranan45 vector correspondence, from across 313 distinct vectors, given possible distinct vectors of $3.52 * 10^{13}$. It was through the application of the probability equation presented in (1) that I would have calculated the likelihood of such an event occurring by chance.

The larger the number of PCs relative to the ECs, the smaller the probability of an EC vector and Sranan45 vector match occurring by chance. If an SED locality with an EC corresponding to the Sranan45 were found, then the probability of this being by chance would be calculated using the formula presented in (1).

(1) Calculating Probability of an EC Vector and Sranan45 Vector Match being a By-chance Occurrence

$$(p)\text{robability} = \frac{\text{ExistingCombinations (EC)}}{\text{PossibleCombinations (PC)}} = (p) = \frac{\text{(EC)}}{3.52 * 10^{13}}$$

3.4.3.2 Calculating probability of a mono-dialectal origin (Partial matches)

There was no instance of a full SED45~Sranan45 correspondence found in the data. There were, however, partial matches (see Chapter 4) and so I had to revise the probability calculations to deal with partial matches and what they could tell us about the English input in Sranan. To this end (Cran) R's pbinom function was utilised. The pbinom function was useful for summing consecutive binomial probabilities, which is what the partial matches represented (Larget 2007). Let me explain the inner workings of the pbinom function. Consider, that during the time of investigation of the SED45~Sranan45 correspondence data, an imaginary coin was taken and used to construct each (EC) vector of 45 matches and non-matches as a series of 45 independent coin tosses. This rendered my experiment to be a binomial one, by virtue of the fact that:

1. the coin was tossed for each of the 45 items;

2. the result of each toss was either a "heads", i.e. [+match] (which is equal to p) with one of the items in the target vector input for the Sranan45, or a "tails", i.e. [–match] with one of the items in the target vector. Failure to get a "heads" on a toss would therefore be equal to $(1 - p)$, i.e. 1 minus the probability of getting a [+match];

3. there was a constant probability of getting [+match] on each of the 45 independent coin tosses, i.e. a 0.5 (50%) chance. The reverse was also true; I had a 0.5 (50%) chance of getting a [–match]. Since each toss of my coin was autonomous, getting a "tails", for example, would not have affected whether I got another "tails", or even "heads" on another toss. On each toss of my coin, the probability of [+match] was equal to (p).

The total number of [+match]'s, (r), therefore had the binomial distribution binom$(45, p)$, with the mean of the distribution equal to $45p$ (total tosses multiplied by the value of p) and variance (how widely the degree of (EC) matches vary across the data), equal to $45p (1 - p)$. Therefore, with the p value in hand, the number of matches (t) was calculated, such that the chance of $p(r \geq t)$ that the number of matches in a given (EC) vector exceeds the threshold number of matches (t) is small, i.e. < 0.05 (see Chapter 4). If the (p) value was found to be less than the threshold (t), i.e. then it could be said that the probability of partial matches was not "by-chance". It would be possible to then determine what level of partial matching would be statistically significant as it related to the partially matching (EC) vector(s) of input for the Sranan45 (see Chapter 4) by using the following calculation in R:

(2) Calculating Probability partial matches being by-chance
```
fp = function(p) (pbinom(t, 45, p) - tails/ec)^2
optimize (fp, c(0,1))
```

What the first line of the formula in (2) calculated, via the binom function in R, was the binomial probability of (threshold number of matches, given 45 independent trials, and p) subtracted from the tails probability of remaining EC vectors divided by the overall number of EC vectors, all squared (see Chapter 4). The second line of the formula used the optimize function of R to search the interval (SED45) for a minimum or maximum with respect to fp (calculated from the first line of the formula) given the condition (c), 0 equals [–match] and 1, [+match], with a probability of getting either a 0 or a 1 being .5 (50%).

3.4.4 Dialect geography (Component 2 of the assessment tool)

The results from this (statistical) component of the proposed methodological model were disregarded temporarily and the correspondence data were then assessed via the Dialect geography component of the analytical tool. At this level of analysis I attempted to access the probability of the English input for the Sranan45, originating from dialects all over England, as opposed to one dialect or group of geographically related dialect areas.

3.4.4.1 Assessing the possibility of pan-dialectal sources: Linguistic feature mapping

The assumption behind this approach is that a mono-dialectal origin will produce a concentrated geographic area for matches with the Sranan45, whereas a pan-dialectal origin will produce not concentrated area of matches.

The geographical distributions of the corresponding language forms, identified between the SED45 word variants and the Sranan45 reflexes, were plotted on computer generated, SED-survey-based, dialectal maps of England. Concentric circles of 1cm (27 km) apart were drawn on these maps from the core locality in regions to the north, east, south and west of England, respectively. These core localities were identified based on the extent to which, for each dialect region, they exhibited the highest degree of correspondence to the Sranan45. These circles were drawn until all localities providing the relevant putative input variants, needed by the core locality to complete the 45 putative input variants, were secured. The rationale behind this is discussed in the following paragraph.

The core locality with the smallest outermost circle would be taken as the area of putative input. This is because a distribution with the shortest radius in all directions, in which all the putative input forms are secured, would equate to the densest dialectal concentration of the relevant cognates for the Sranan45 reflexes. In this regard, should the localities forming this dense distribution of the input be concentrated in one region, i.e. whether in the north, east, south or west of England – or a specific county within one of these regions – then that geographic space would represent the input area of origin. However, should the distribution(s) of the input, irrespective of whichever core locality we start from, present us with outermost circles of equal or near equal radii (in all directions), spanning different regions, it could then be concluded that the etyma for the Sranan45 reflexes originated from all over England (see Chapter 5).

Corroboration of the results of the statistical analysis by this alternative approach, i.e. linguistic feature mapping, would represent confirmation for an identified input from two independent levels of analysis. Lack of corroboration could result if:

1. the linguistic feature mapping pinpointed no dialectal concentration of input forms, but a distribution from all over England;

2. the linguistic feature mapping highlighted a concentrated distribution of the input forms in a dialect or group of geographically related dialects that was/were not identified in the statistical analysis.

If scenario 1 occured this could simply mean that the results of the statistical analysis highlighted a potential input area or group of areas that the dialect geography failed to identify. If scenario 2 was true, then it could mean that the linguistic feature mapping highlighted an input area or group of areas that the statistical analysis did not identify. What was in fact highlighted from the data, at this level of analysis is: (1) corroboration of one aspect of the results of the statistical component and non-corroboration of another and (2) the identification of an input area that was not highlighted via the statistical component of analysis (see Chapter 5). At this point, I had already succeeded, in my mind, in showing the value of using my proposed tripartite method of analysis. This is because where one component of analysis had failed to identify an input area, the other component of analysis did not. This approach was further strengthened by the historical component of analysis, which offered confirmation for the results of both the statistical and linguistic feature mapping components of analysis. The results at this level of analysis, i.e. the historical level (see §3.4.5), indicated that migrants from those areas pinpointed by both the statistical analysis and linguistic feature mapping, were going to the relevant place(s) at the relevant time(s), to provide the putative input for the Sranan45 reflexes (see Chapter 6).

3.4.5 Historical analysis (Component 3 of the assessment tool)

This current study, as alluded to above, triangulated the results from the statistical linguistic analysis and the geo-linguistic mapping, with 17th century historical data concerning migration patterns from England to the Americas. However, unlike the two previous components of analysis, i.e. the statistical and the geo-linguistic feature mapping, the Sranan45 and SED45 data were not directly consulted at this level of analysis. This is because it was only the locality(ies) pinpointed by these two components of analyses that were of importance.

What was attempted at the historical level of analysis, was to answer three questions regarding migration from England, during the time of Suriname's settlement by the English and subsequent cession to the Dutch. These questions were as follows:

1. Can we establish a chain of migration from England to Suriname, between the years 1650 and 1667?

2. Can we establish a chain of migration from England, within the same time span mentioned in (a.), to the English colonies in the Caribbean and subsequently Suriname?

3. If the answer to (a.) and/or (b.) is in the affirmative, then what percentage of the total number of migrants to the Caribbean, including Suriname, is from the localities identified from the statistical analysis and geo-linguistic feature mapping?

To answer these questions three major types of historical data were assessed (see §3.2.3):

1. The origins of the British indentured servants to Barbados and other Caribbean colonies from which Suriname is settled,

2. Governors and big planters of Suriname and their origins in England,

3. The English geographical origin of "His Majesty's servants", leaving Suriname for Jamaica after its cession to the Dutch in 1667.

The rationale behind this approach was fairly simple. The historical analysis would confirm the presence of migrants from the locality(ies) highlighted by the statistical and dialect geography analyses or highlight other areas missed by the first two components of analysis. There is also the possibility, as alluded to in §3.4.4.1, which is that either one or both of the first two components of analysis pinpointed dialect areas that the historical analysis might have failed to highlight.

3.4.6 Integrated findings and conclusion

The amalgamated findings from all three components of analysis were then used to construct the tale of the English input in Sranan and by extension of English migrants in Suriname. This tale involves concepts of dialect levelling and koinei-sation, of settlement and cession and of input that is not from all over England but from specific dialects whose influences are explained by numbers of migrants, alongside the social status of an emerging Standard English (see Chapter 7). The overall process, presented in this chapter, which led to this tale of input, is con-densed into the Research Process Chart in Figure 3.1 on page 57.

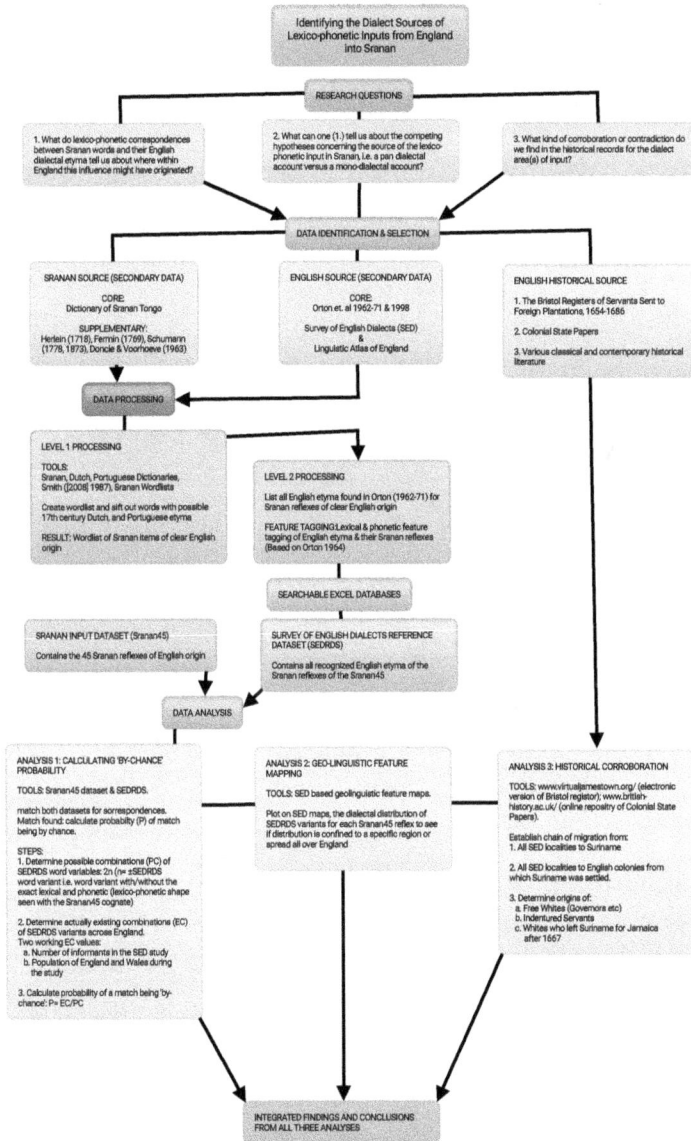

Figure 3.1: Research process chart

4 Testing probability of origin

4.1 Introduction

This chapter is a demonstration of the statistical analysis of the degree of correspondence between the SED45 and the Sranan45. It is a presentation of what this degree of correspondence says about the extent to which a mono-dialectal account of origin is probable. In Chapter 3, I presented the formula with which I calculated this probability as $P = EC/PC$. This meant that if I found a single SED45 locality of 100% correspondence with the Sranan45, the (P)robability of this being a by chance occurrence would be calculated as the existing combinations (EC) of vectors divided by the total number of possible combinations (PC) of vectors in the SED45.

The above-mentioned formula would have been relevant if any (EC) vector in the SED45 provided a 100% match with the Sranan45 vector. However, as mentioned in Chapter 3, what the data presented, were partial matches. These partial matches ranged from a high of 60% ($^{27}/_{45}$) to a low of 20% ($^{9}/_{45}$). I therefore needed to revert to the secondary formula discussed in Chapter 3 (see §3.4.3.2), which could be used to calculate the statistical significance of these matches and by extension the probability of these partial matches, in particular the ($^{27}/_{45}$) match, being a by chance occurrence. Before delving into the discussion of these partial matches, let me first discuss how the old probability formula, which deals with total matches, would have worked.

4.1.1 Calculating the possible combinations figure (PC)

For any dataset containing horizontally ordered sequences of variants of the SED45 word variables, there are two possibilities:

1. There is specific combination of eight linguistic features (see §3.3.2 in Chapter 3) across the 45 items in the SED45. In this case we can say that a "match" with the items in the Sranan45 has occurred. To illustrate this, take the putative SED45 sequence [ars] *arse*, [hɒg] *hog* and [kəʊld] *cold*, produced in

Earl's Croome (Worcestershire) and compare it with the sequence of Sranan45 reflexes [ras], [hagu] and [kouru]. The words [ars] and [ras] match with +PVR, [hɒg] and [hagu] match with +h and +LexVar and [kəʊld] and [kouru] both match with the +Diph.

2. There is a different combination, in which case we can say that a "non-match" has occurred. Using the same hypothetical sequence above, a non-match would occur if the SED45 sequence was [aːs], [hɒg] and [kəʊld], as produced, for example, in Witton-le-Wear (Durham). This non-match would be with the variant [aːs] *arse*, which needs to have the +PVR feature to be taken as the input etymon for the Sranan45 reflex [ras].

Given these two possibilities, we can think of the SED45 with their 45 SED items, as an ordered vector of length 45 SED word variants, with each SED word variant being either [+match] or [−match] with its corresponding Sranan45 reflex. In using this binary system of categorization, the number of possible distinct combinations is calculated as 2^{45} (see 1).

(1) Possible combinations (PC) of the variants of the SED45 Variables:

$$2^{45} = 3.52 * 10^{13}$$

This equates to a little over 35 trillion distinct vectors (PC).

4.1.2 Calculating the existing combinations figure (EC)

A count of the number of localities, out of the 313 surveyed in the SED, which in the SED45 database exhibited distinct variant combinations across the SED45 etyma, revealed that with the exception of two localities, every SED locality had its own distinct vector. The one case of two locations producing the same vector of 45 variants involved neighbouring locations Ullesthorpe and Carlton Curlieu, both in Leicestershire. This meant that, as it related to the actually Existing Combinations (EC), of the variants in the SED45, there are 312 distinct vectors (EC). I could now calculate the Probability of a full (EC) Sranan45 target vector correspondence being a by chance occurrence, given that there are 312 (EC)s and over 35 trillion distinct vector combinations (PC)s.

4.1.3 Calculating probability (P)

Having secured the (EC) value and the (EC) value, we would then apply the statistical procedure that establishes the level of probability of the required Sranan45 combination corresponding by chance with an actual (EC) in the SED45. We calculate the following probability. There are $N = 3.52 * 10^{13}$ PC vectors, and there are $k = 312$ EC vectors. In addition to these, there is the "target vector" that represents the precise SED input for the Sranan45 vector. The probability of this "target vector" being one of the (EC) vectors is simply k/N, i.e. EC/PC. This probability is therefore:

(2) Calculating probability of an EC Vector and Sranan45 vector match being a by-chance occurrence:

$$\frac{312}{3.52 * 10^{13}} = 8.86 * 10^{-12}$$

This is a probability of 886 in 1 trillion.

(2) illustrates that given the large number of possible combinations of the 45 word variables, it is highly unlikely that finding an (EC) vector that matched the "target vector", i.e. an SED45 vector combination that exhibits a 100% match with the Sranan45, would have been a by chance event. As mentioned above, however, no such (EC) vector exists in the SED45 database. What exist in the database are 312 (EC) vectors which display partial matches with the target vector, exhibited in the Sranan45 database. We will now go into the discussion of these partial matches and the statistical tool, R, which was used to calculate the statistical significance of getting these partial matches and whether this was by chance.

4.2 Calculating probability (P) for partial matches

The probability calculations of the partial matches presented hereafter were undertaken using the statistical analysis tool R (see §3.4.3.2). I inputted the SED45 and Sranan45 vectors into this computing environment and asked R to determine the level of statistical significance, with Alpha level 5% (see §4.2.1 for discussion of Alpha), of the partial matches between the (EC) vectors in the SED45 database and the Sranan45. R's built-in pbinom function, which is used in the calculation of the partial matches, was then utilized. This pbinom function is useful for summing consecutive binomial probabilities (Lagart 2007), which the partial matches' data represented. Before going any further into the discussion of binomial probability, let me explain the concept of Alpha level.

4.2.1 Alpha (type I error)

The following discussion of Alpha is based on the California State University's webpage presentation on *"Tests for Significance"*, last modified on April 22, 1998 (Lagart 2007), and Cowles & Davis (1982) article *"On the Origins of the .05 Level of Statistical Significance"*. If a researcher thinks that there is a relationship between two variables under investigation but the evidence says otherwise, then s/he has committed a Type I error. The probability of committing this type of error is referred to as "Alpha". Researchers will most often specify the Alpha level that they are willing to accept. In the social sciences and areas of statistics the Alpha level of .05 is most often chosen. This equates to a willingness to accept a 5% probability of making a Type I error of assuming a relationship between two variables when no such relationship exists. I opted to also use an Alpha level of .05. I did so, on the premise that if the relationship between the two vectors, i.e. the target vector for the Sranan45 and the partial matching (EC) vectors was strong (not by chance) or not (by chance), then with a small sample size of 312 (EC)s, an Alpha level of .05 would detect this.

In light of the above discussion I not only looked at the highest matching (EC) vector, exhibited by the lect of Blagdon, with its 60% match. I included those localities whose (EC) vectors of partial matches ranged from $^{22}/_{45}$ to $^{27}/_{45}$, i.e. EC vector matches $\geq$ 48.89% (see Table 4.1). These lower end matches were included since they satisfied the Alpha level of .05 (see §4.2.2).

Table 4.1: SED Localities with $\geq$ $^{22}/_{45}$ matches with the Sranan45 target vector

Localities	/45
Stogursey (Somersetshire), Pulham St. Mary (Norfolk), Yoxford (Suffolk), Netheravon (Wiltshire), Whitechurch Canonicorum (Dorsetshire), Earl's Croome & Hartlebury (Worcestershire), Latterbridge & Gretton (Gloucestershire), Little Bentley and Tillingham (Essex), Outwood and Walton-on-Hill (Surrey)	22
East Mersea, Doddinghurst and Canewdon (Essex)	23
Wedmore and Horsington (Somersetshire)	24
Whitwell I.O.W. (Hampshire)	25
Blagdon (Somersetshire)	27

4.2.2 Binomial probability

In Chapter 3, I used the analogy of flipping an imaginary coin. Let us take out this imaginary coin again and go through the steps I went through in working with the partial matches data. Each (EC) vector of 45 matches and non-matches was constructed as a series of 45 independent coin tosses. In so doing the experiment became a binomial experiment because:

1. R was asked to autonomously toss the coin for each of 45 items, per 312 SED localities;

2. R gave either heads, i.e. [+match] (which is equal to p) with one of the items in the target vector of the Sranan45, or tails, i.e. [−match] with one of the items in the target vector. This failure to get heads on a toss was calculated as $(1 - p)$, i.e. 1 minus the probability of getting a [+match];

3. I had a constant probability, i.e. 0.5 (50%), of getting [+match] on each of the 45 independent tosses of the coin;

4. Each coin toss was autonomous, so getting tails, for example, did not affect whether I got another tails, or even heads on another spin of the coin.

On each toss of our coin, the probability of a [+match] was equal to P. The total number of [+match]'s (r), i.e. 22, 23, ... 27, would therefore have the binomial distribution binom$(45, p)$, with the "mean" of the distribution equal to $45p$ (total tosses times the value of p) and "variance", i.e. how widely the degree of (EC) matches vary across the data, equal to $45p(1-p)$. I therefore needed the value of p, with which it would be straightforward to calculate the threshold (minimum → maximum) number of matches (t), i.e. 22 → 27, such that the probability $p(r \geq t)$ that the number of matches (r), in a given (EC) vector exceeded the threshold number of matches (t), was small, i.e. < 0.05 (less than 5%). If this P value was less than the threshold (t) I could then say that the probability of getting partial matches was in no way a by chance occurrence. If I found any locality with a P value > .05, then I would conclude that the partial matching of such a locality was a by chance occurrence.

In applying this to the data, let us say that when I asked the SED45 database if an SED item yielded a match in two varieties, the probability P of a match was equal to X number. I already knew that there were 45 items in each of the 313 SED varieties and my knowing this could therefore have been compared to a situation in which my imaginary coin was biased, with P(heads) = X number (a baseline number that I still needed to calculate); I tossed the coin 45 times. For each time the coin reached the ground, I got (r) number of (heads) matches across the 45 features, across the 45 tosses. Two questions could have been asked from this coin tossing exercise:

1. What is $p(r = 22$ matches), i.e. what is the probability that the total number of matches is $^{22}\!/_{45}$?

2. What is $p(r \geq 22$ matches) i.e. what is the probability that the total number of matches is equal to or greater than $^{22}\!/_{45}$?

Question 1, i.e. $p(r =$ exactly 22 matches), was not the most interesting to ask. However, getting an answer to Question 2 would prove to be more interesting. This is because on one hand, the event ($r = 22$) is contained within the event ($r \geq 22$), and on the other hand, the latter event, i.e. ($r \geq 22$), led me to ask and attempt to answer two other important and interrelated questions. These were as follows:

1. What is a remarkably "large" number of SED45 to Sranan45 matches? The answer is "large" $= r >$ some number (t), i.e. threshold, such that the probability of this "large" value occurring by chance is "small", i.e. < 0.05 as discussed above.

2. What is the number of matches, such that $p(r \geq t)$ is < 0.05? The SED45 and Sranan45 data were inputted into R and the SED45 data were asked the following two questions as it related to its degree of matching with the Sranan45 target vector: "What is the threshold number of matches (t), such that if an observed vector (EC) has more than (t) matches i.e. 22, 23, 24, ... 27, we could say that such an event is unlikely to have occurred by chance?" In particular, "is the observation of Blagdon's $^{27}\!/_{45}$ match an "unlikely" event under the chance hypothesis, and strong evidence in favour of the hypothesis that the Blagdon dialect is the source of the target vector for the Sranan45 reflexes?" Before R could calculate this request there was a need to construct an approximate model for the varying distribution of matches illustrated in Table 4.1.

A simple estimate of p was taken as the proportion of all vector elements that were [+match] between the SED45 and the target vector, which is exhibited by the Sranan45 reflexes. Using the degree of matches across the data in the SED45, an estimate for p was calculated as follows:

1. Start with the low proportion of vectors having $^{21}\!/_{45}$ or fewer matches, which is equivalent to $^{292}\!/_{313}$, i.e. the non-matches (tails figure) of 292 (EC)s out the actual 313 in the data.

2. Equate this probability to the lower tails probability of $b(45, p)$; this resulted in the equation below:

(3) Securing an estimate for P
```
fp = functionP (pbinom(21, 45, p) - 292/313)^2
optimize (fp, c(0,1))
$minimum
[1] 0.367463
```

What the formula in (3) calculated was a value for p within the event (21 [+match]es, from out of 45 independent trials, minus the tails figure of $^{292}\!/_{313}$, remaining (non-matching) vectors, all squared), where the conditions, based on the structure of the data, are that there is 0.5 chance of getting a 0, i.e. [−match], and a 0.5 chance of getting a 1, i.e. [+match]. The result, which is equivalent to the minimum threshold value between $22 \rightarrow 27$, was $p = 0.367463$. R's optimize function was used to do this since it yields the value that minimizes a function over a specified interval, i.e. $22 \rightarrow 27$ in this case. The resulting estimate for P made it possible to ask R to calculate $p(r \geq t)$, for $t = 22, 23, ..., 27$. This was done as follows:

(4) Calculating $p(r \geq t)$ (see 3 for the calculation for p0)
```
$Objective # (this is the value of functionP at maximum)
$[1] 2.800027^-10
p0 = 0.367463
1 - pbinom(c (21:26), 45, p0)
# which is:
1 - pbinom(c (21:26), 45, 0.367463)
```

The resulting probabilities of the calculations illustrated in (4), i.e. $p(r \geq t)$ for $t = 22, 23, ..., 27$, were as follows:

These calculations, using the approximate model, suggested that $^{23}\!/_{45}$ matches or more might be regarded as unusually high at the 5% significance level. This corresponded to vectors with more than 50% matches. Based on the calculations presented in Table 4.2, the list of localities presented in Table 4.1 was reduced

Table 4.2: Results of the calculation for $p(r \geq t)$

(t) Threshold	Probabilities
22	0.0641
23	0.0343
24	0.0170
25	0.0078
26	0.0033
27	0.0013

to only those SED localities whose (EC) to Sranan45 correspondence was unusually high (statistically significant) at the 5% significance level. The following localities were removed from the list: Stogursey (Somersetshire), Pulham St. Mary (Norfolk), Yoxford (Suffolk), Netheravon (Wiltshire), Whitechurch Canonicorum (Dorsetshire), Earl's Croome and Hartlebury (Worcestershire), Latterbridge and Gretton (Gloucestershire), Little Bentley and Tillingham (Essex), and Outwood and Walton-on-Hill (Surrey). All of them exhibited matches of $^{22}/_{45}$. Having excluded these thirteen localities, I was left with seven localities with (EC) vectors exhibiting > 50% correspondence with the Sranan45 reflexes. These localities are presented in Table 4.3.

Table 4.3: SED Localities with > 50% Matches with the Sranan45 Target Vector

Localities	/45	P
East Mersea, Doddinghurst and Canewdon (Essex)	23	.0343
Wedmore and Horsington (Somersetshire)	24	.0170
Whitwell I.O.W (Hampshire)	25	.0078
Blagdon (Somersetshire)	27	.0013

Table 4.3 highlights the fact that the Blagdon (EC) has an almost six times lower probability, i.e. 0.0013, of its partial correspondence being "by chance" than does Whitwell Isle of White (Hampshire). Whitwell Isle of White, hereafter I.O.W., has the second lowest by chance score of 0.0078. Blagdon has an almost thirteen times lower probability than the third set of localities, i.e. Wedmore and Horsington (Somersetshire), with their probability of 0.0170. Blagdon also has about twenty-six times lower probability of its partial matching being by chance than does

the fourth set of localities; i.e. East Mersea, Doddinghurst and Canewdon (Essex) with their 0.0343 probability. Consequently, Blagdon, with its 0.0013 probability of its 60% ($^{27}/_{45}$) match with the target vector not being by change, stood out as the most statistically likely source of the Sranan45 reflexes.

The high statistically significant probabilities exhibited by the six remaining localities could not be neglected however, since all six 'not by chance' localities, i.e. Whitwell i.o.w., Wedmore, Horsington, East Mersea, Doddinghurst and Canewdon, could also be considered potential sources for the Sranan45. Consider two further facts concerning these remaining six localities:

- three of these seven localities, i.e. East Mersea, Doddinghurst and Canewdon, are situated in the East and East Anglia region of England, specifically in the same county of Essex;

- the remaining three, i.e. Whitwell, i.o.w. (Hampshire), Horsington and Wedmore (Somersetshire), are alongside Blagdon, situated in the western part of the south of England.

One question came to mind when I noticed this pattern. This question was as follows: "is there a linguistic relatedness between the south and east of England and if so what does it tell us about the nature of the English dialectal input into Sranan?" Trying to decipher this tale of potential linguistic relatedness would involve my looking at the degree of linguistic overlap between these seven localities. The steps taken to answer the question of linguistic relatedness are discussed in detail in Chapter 7.

4.3 Assessment of the results of the statistical analysis

The results of the statistical analysis pinpointed a statistical significant lect – Blagdon (Somersetshire), albeit with a partial match, i.e. $^{27}/_{45}$, with the Sranan45 target vector. However, though Blagdon was identified as being the most statistically significant putative input lect, six other lects were presented as being of near statistical significance to Blagdon's 60% correspondence with the target vector. These lects are situated to the east of England, specifically in Essex in East Anglia and the south of England, specifically in Somersetshire and Hampshire. These results presented me with two possibilities:

Possibility 1: Blagdon, being the most statistically significant input was the input lect for the Sranan45. Its remaining 40% ($^{18}/_{45}$) non-correspondences with the Sranan45 might therefore be attributed to internal and external language change overtime. This possibility seemed worthy of serious consideration, since the SED was conducted over 300 years from the period of interest, which is from 1650 to 1667 (see Chapter 6).

Problem: I did not want to make any hasty conclusions, especially because possibility 1 fails to account for the remaining six localities whose partial matches could also be attributed to internal and external language changes over the 300-year period. This means that any one, if not all of the seven localities, i.e. Blagdon, Whitwell, Wedmore, Horsington, Canewdon, Doddinghurst and East Mersea, could have possibly been the input for the Sranan45.

Possibility 2: The input for the Sranan45 was from two major regions in which there was a group of localities in close geographical proximity, with one of these localities forming the core of the linguistic influence. This possibility seemed very feasible since I could essentially cluster the seven localities of statistical significance, according to region and the counties within these regions, in which each locality is located (see Chapter 5).

Problem: Possibility 2 seemed to be the more viable of the two possibilities. This was particularly because the seven localities formed two non-contiguous clusters; these being Blagdon, Horsington, Whitwell, Wedmore in the south of England and Canewdon, Doddinghurst and East Mersea in the east and East Anglia region. Still, as with possibility 1, I did not want to jump to conclusions.

Given the problems with the two possibilities presented above I wanted to assess the SED45~Sranan45 correspondence data anew, via an alternative approach, i.e. via the use of Linguistic Feature Mapping. I wanted to see if in using this alternative approach, I would arrive at results that would corroborate, add to, or disconfirm the results of the statistical analysis that were presented in this chapter.

5 A dialect geography approach

5.1 Introduction

I discussed, in Chapter 4, the statistical probability of a mono-dialectal account of origin for the Sranan45 and the fact that the results of that analysis favoured seven input localities with statistically significant degrees of 'not by chance' matching with the Sranan45. These areas are Blagdon, Whitwell, Wedmore, Horsington, Canewdon, Doddinghurst and East Mersea. These results presented me with the possibility that the input for the Sranan45 was from two regional dialect groups (see Table 5.1).

Table 5.1: Regional distribution of the seven lects of statistical significance

Southern England Dialect Group	East and East Anglia Dialect Group
Sommersetshire	**Essex**
Blagdon	Doddinghurst
Wedmore	East Mersea
Horsington	Horsington
Hampshire	
Withwell (Isle of White)	

Table 5.1 highlights the fact that the input for the Sranan45, based on the results of the statistical analysis presented in Chapter 4, was possibly a composite dialect whose features originated from localities in the south and in the east and East Anglia regions of England. Let us see what the distribution highlighted in Table 5.1, looks like on a map of England (see Figure 5.1 on following page).

Figure 5.1: Distribution of the 7 localities of high statistical significance

5.2 Linguistic feature mapping

The results of the statistical analysis presented in the previous chapter were disregarded and the SED45 data was subjected to the dialect geography component of analysis. In so doing, the data was used to create geo-linguistic feature mappings of the forty-five putative input forms across England. There were two reasons of using this dialect geography approach. First, it was a means by which to disconfirm/confirm the results of the statistical analysis. Second, it helped in addressing another possibility that had to be considered; i.e. that the results of the statistical calculations did not account for all conceivable scenarios pointing to the origin(s) of the putative input for the Sranan45 input. To this end, it was hypothesised that the Sranan45 putative input from England might have come from converged dialects, which might or might not have been situated in the same regional geographic space. Consequently, via the linguistic feature mapping of the forty-five putative input etyma it would be possible to determine whether there were clusters of localities, which might exhibit denser distributions of the putative input forms than that which might be noticed with Blagdon and its surrounding localities in the south of England.

This hypothesis of converged dialects is referred to the *Regional Input Hypothesis*. This chapter is a presentation of the steps taken to test this hypothesis, the results of this assessment and the degree of corroboration between the conclusions arrived at in comparison to the results of the statistical analysis presented in Chapter 4.

5.3 Assessing the regional input hypothesis

The Regional Input Hypothesis, hereafter RIH, was as follows: "the geo-linguistic source in England, of the SED45 input etyma relevant to the formation of the Sranan45, was possibly a specific region, i.e. North, South, East and East Anglia, and, West and West Midlands, in which there was a core dialect locality of major linguistic influence." If this were true, then a geo-linguistic mapping of the forty-five putative SED45 input etyma would reveal a dense regional distribution of localities in close geographic proximity to this core locality. The above divisions of England were based on how Orton et al. (1962–71) sectionalised England for the SED survey.

5.4 Dialect mapping

The soundness of the RIH was assessed by drawing Concentric Circles of 1cm (27 km) apart, on a SED-inspired map of England, from the locality in the northern, east and East Anglia, west and West Midlands, and southern regions of England, whose SED45 (EC) vector demonstrated the highest levels of correspondence with the Sranan45 target vector, within their respective region. These four regions were selected in accordance with the way in which Orton et al. (1962–71) sectionalised England into regions for the Survey of English Dialects, undertaken between 1950 and 1961 (see §3.2.2.1). These localities of high correspondence in the four regions, i.e. north, west and West Midlands, east and East Anglia, and south, were referred to as Start Lects, SL for short. I took as the region of influence for the Sranan45, any region that fulfilled one major criterion, i.e. that this region's distribution of the relevant features produced the smallest outermost circle in which all of the forty-five putative SED45 input etyma are found. An additional characteristic of this criterion was that there was no requirement to move outside of the particular region to secure any variant. The localities situated within this circle would therefore be deemed to be the regional input source for the Sranan45.

5.4.1 Map conventions and approach

The map of England that was used in the linguistic feature mapping was created through a PHP (Hypertext Pre-processor) script, a simple but powerful scripting language used in webpage creation. In an email message, dated February 22, 2010, its creator Dieter Studer explained that he fashioned the base map by copying the outline of the base map in Viereck's *Computer-Developed Linguistic Atlas of*

England (Viereck 1990). The localities surveyed in the SED were plotted on the map via the imaging functionality of PHP using the same x- and y- values from Viereck (1990). Viereck's Computer-Developed Linguistic Atlas of England, "... is the first computer-developed linguistic atlas of England... [whose] ... database is that provided by the Survey of English Dialects ..." (Viereck 1997: 79).

A scale was created for my version of Studer's map, by using the known distance of two locations in England, i.e. the distance between Birmingham and London. This is approximately 160.9 km, which is equivalent to 6 cm on the map used in this research. The distance between each 1 cm-apart Concentric Circle drawn on the map is therefore equivalent to approximately 27 km on land.

5.4.1.1 Start lects

In each of the four regions of England the distribution of the Start Lects of highest correspondence with the Sranan45 reflexes were as follows:

1. North: Wearhead, Brigham and Wark with $^{21}/_{45}$ (47%);

2. West and West Midlands: Hartlebury, Latterbridge, Earl's Croome and Grenton with $^{22}/_{45}$ (49%);

3. East and East Anglia: Doddinghurst, Canewdon and East Mersea with $^{23}/_{45}$ (51%);

4. South: Blagdon with $^{27}/_{45}$ (60%).

The first three regions, i.e. the north, west and east & East Anglia of England, posed a problem. Several localities in these regions attained the highest regional score, albeit with different combinations of the forty-five SED45 putative input etyma for the Sranan45. This issue of competing distributions was dealt with by selecting from among the competing localities in each region, the locality that required the smallest circle to include the other competing areas (see Figures 5.2–5.4).

As illustrated in the Figure 5.2, potential SL Wearhead (purple) exhibited the smallest circle in which the other two potential SLs for the north of England were captured. Wearhead's radius is 102.06 km (3.78 cm); the other two potential SLs, i.e. Wark and Brigham, have a radius of 121.5 km (4.5 cm) and 135 km (5 cm), respectively.

As illustrated in the Figure 5.3, potential SL Earl's Croome (purple) exhibited the smallest circle in which the other two potential SL candidates for the west and West Midlands of England are captured. Earl's Croome's radius is 110.7 km

Figure 5.2: Optimal start lect candidate: North of England

(4.1 cm); the other two potential SLs, i.e. Hartlebury and Latterbridge, both have
a radius of 162 km (6 cm). Let us now look at the optimal SL candidate for the east
and East Anglia.

As illustrated in the Figure 5.4, potential SL Canewdon (purple) exhibited the
smallest circle in which the other two potential SLs for the east and East Anglia of
England were captured. Canewdon's radius is 72.9 km (2.7 cm); the other two potential SLs, i.e. Doddinghurst and East Mersea, have a radius of 108 km (4 cm) and
124.2 km (4.6 cm), respectively. This selection process left me with the following
SLS:

1. North: SL Wearhead with $^{21}/_{45}$;

2. West and West Midlands: SL Earl's Croome with $^{22}/_{45}$;

3. East and East Anglia: SL Canewdon with $^{23}/_{45}$;

4. South: SL Blagdon with $^{27}/_{45}$.

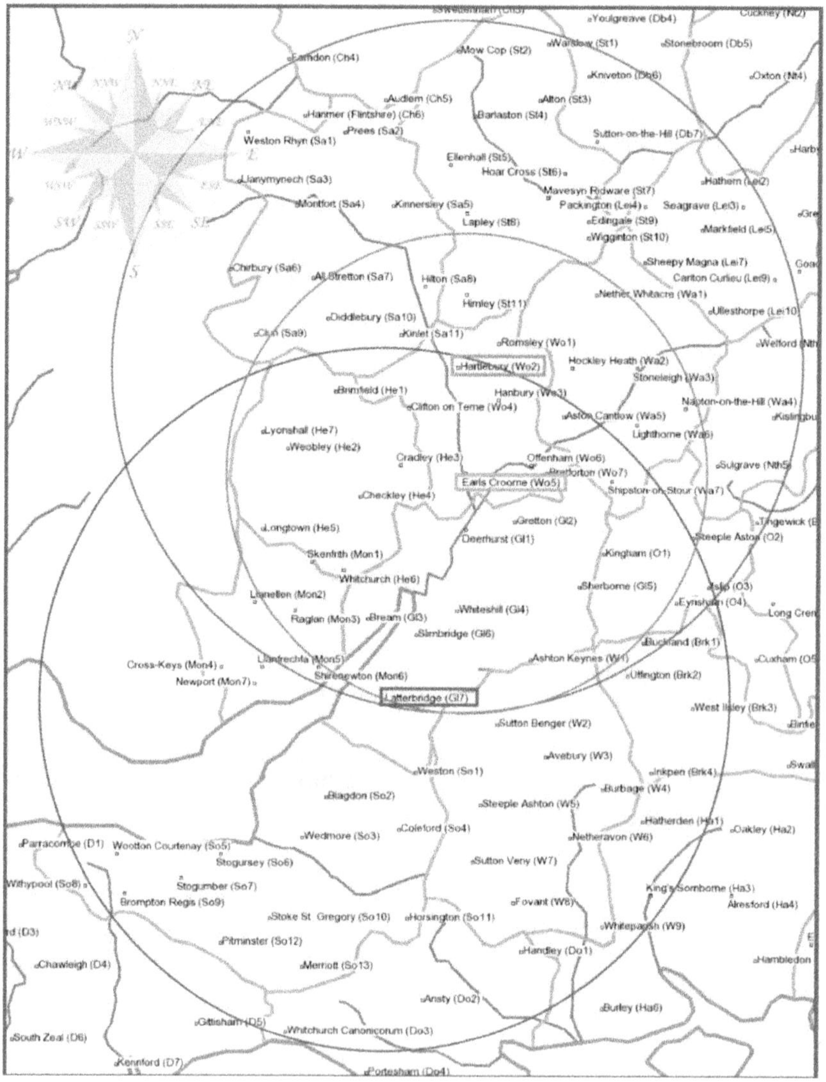

Figure 5.3: Optimal start sect candidate: West and West Midlands of England

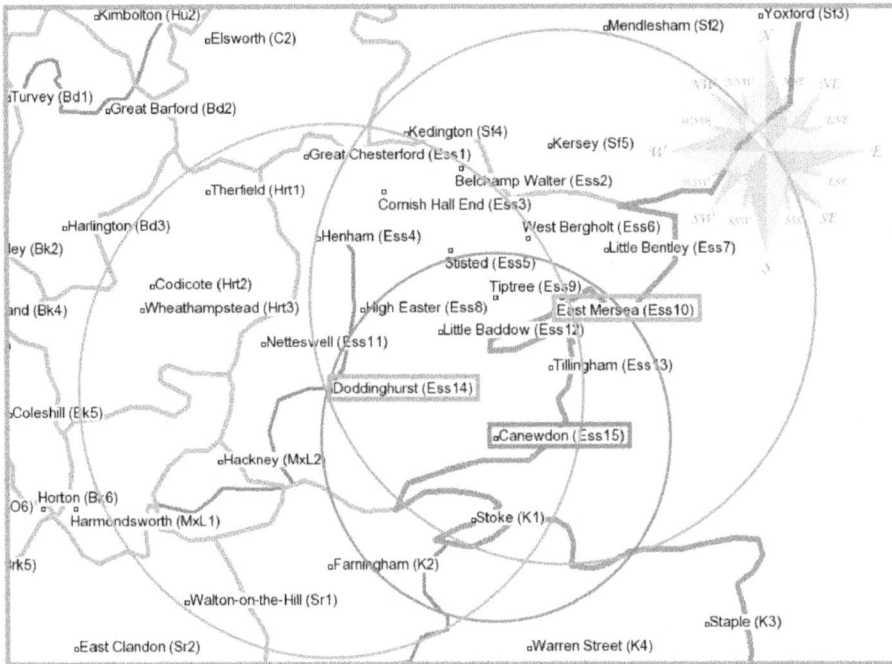

Figure 5.4: Optimal start lect candidate: East and East Anglia of England

Having identified these four regional SLs the next step was to use Concentric Circles of 1 cm (27 km) apart, going outwards from Wearhead in the north, Canewdon in the east and East Anglia, Earl's Croome in the west and Blagdon in the south, until all relevant SED45 input variants for the Sranan45 were secured. In taking this approach, I could assess the pan-dialectal account of origin, i.e. whether the origin of the Sranan45 input forms originated from all over England, as would be the case if Mufwene (2008a; 2001) "all over" account of origin were correct (see Chapter 2).

The rationale behind this was that if there is a need to cover the same distance outwards from each SL, within its respective region, to secure the relevant input forms, then this would be strong evidence that the input was from all over England as opposed to my theorized converged regional dialects hypothesis. Consequently, this method of analysis would serve as a means by which to determine whether there were regionally distributed clusters of localities, which exhibited denser distributions of the putative input forms than that which might be noticed with Blagdon and its surrounding localities in the south of England.

5.5 Map work

There are two types of maps and one table used to present the distribution of the putative input beginning from each of the four SLs. These are *Input Variants Distribution Maps*, IVDM for short, *Input Variants Route Distribution Maps*, IVRDM, and *Concentric Circle-by-Concentric Circle Allocation Tables*, hereafter CCAT. In the section hereafter, using the data related to the north of England, an illustration of how these maps and tables were used to organise and display the data is presented. The presentation of the geo-linguistic data for the three remaining regions follows this.

5.5.1 Geo-linguistic distributions

Beginning with the IVDMs, draw Concentric Circles of 1cm (27 km) apart from each SL. Continue outwards on the shortest path to the next nearest lect containing an SED45 variant needed for the Sranan45 target and out again until all the variants are within the circle. Let me illustrate this by presenting the IVDM for the north of England.

The radius of SL Wearhead's distribution is 351 km (13 cm). It seems to span localities in the north, east, west and a portion of the south of England. The next step was to highlight using CCATs, the input items found within the Concentric Circles surrounding each SL and the localities within these circles that exhibited these input forms. A close look at the CCAT for the north, i.e. CCAT1, highlights the exact locality-by-locality distribution of the input items from within the first circle outwards to the final circle (see CCAT1 (Table 5.2)).

Input Variants Route Distribution Maps (IVRDM)s follow each CCAT. IVRDMs are used to depict, based on the information in the CCATs, the locality-to-locality path outwards from each SL to the last locality required to secure all relevant input etyma for the Sranan45 reflexes. On these maps, each SL is highlighted with a star. Take a look at the IVRDM for the north of England (see Figure 5.5b on the following page).

With the exception of the divergence to Harlington (Bedfordshire) and Netteswell (Essex) in the east, the distribution of the SED45 input forms is in actuality, spread across the north and west of England in a line running southwest from Wearhead in the north to Latterbridge in the west. This distribution of the putative input for the Sranan45 is quite dispersed; it is not confined to the north of England alone but takes in areas to the west, east and south of England. If I noticed a near similar distribution from the other SL, i.e. a distribution that spanned all four regions, I could then have safely assumed that the input for the Sranan45

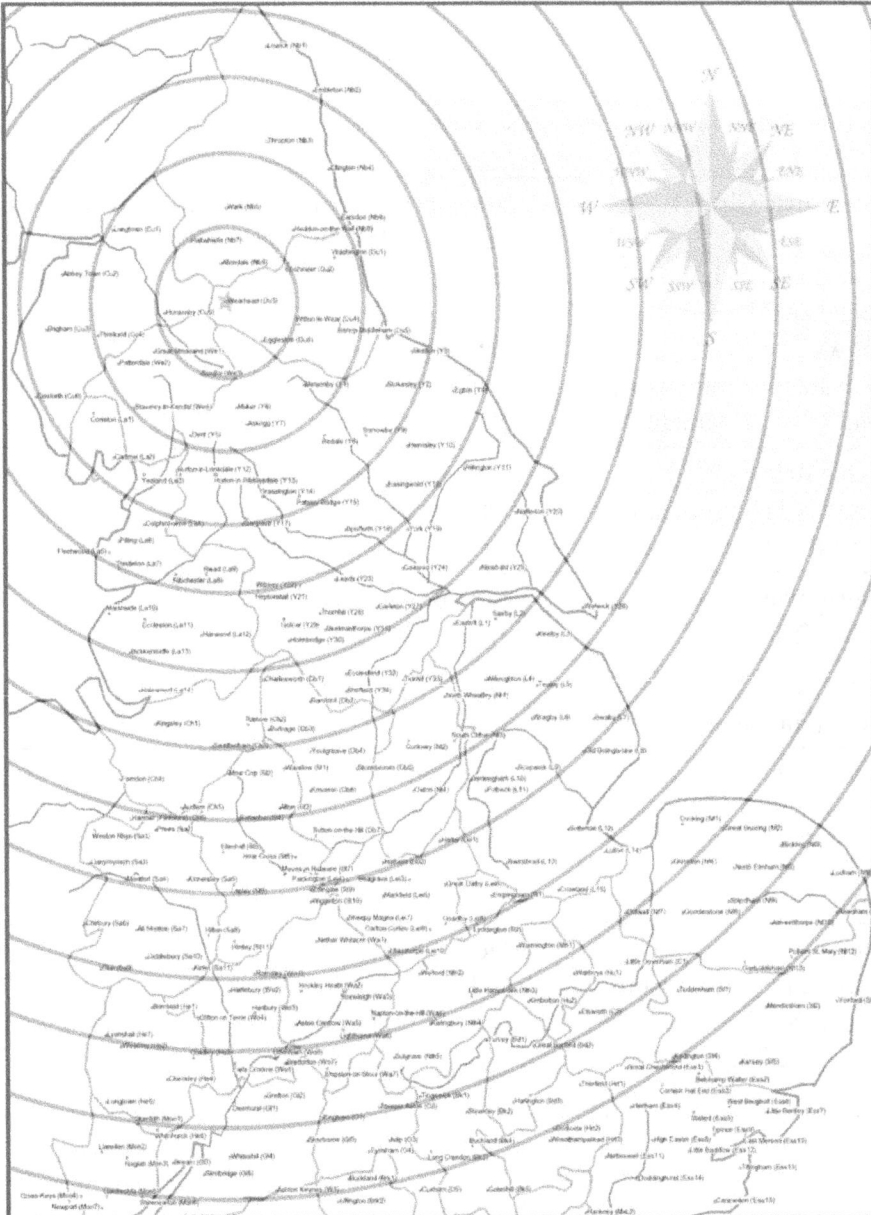

Figure 5.5a: IVDM1: Distribution of remaining putative input items from
SL Wearhead (Northern region)

Table 5.2: CCAT1: Wearhead (Durham) ²¹⁄₄₅ (24 variants to secure)

Concentric Circle1	**arse, broth, corn, remember, turn, care, curse, cold, help, horse, hare**
Ebchester (Durham)	[aʁːs], [bʁɒθ], [kɔʁːn], [ʁɪmɛmbəʁ], [tɔʁːn]
Allendale (Northumberland)	[kȩə], [kɔːs]
Haltwhistle (Northumberland)	[kɔʊld]
Hunsonby (Cumberland)	[hɛlp]
Soulby (Westmoreland)	[hɑs], [hɛː]
Concentric Circle 2	**star, wear, gutter, old**
Longtown (Cumberland)	[staːr], [wɛəɪ]
Wark (Northumberland)	[gʊtʁ], [ɔʊld]
Concentric Circle 3	**herring**
Bedale (Yorkshire)	[jɛɹɪn]
Concentric Circle 5	**hear**
Leeds (Yorkshire)	[jəɹ]
Concentric Circle 8	**eyes, woman**
Llanymynech (Shropshire)	[haɪz], [wʊmən]
Concentric Circle 11	**yesterday**
Longtown (Herefordshire)	[ɛstəɪdɪ]
Concentric Circle 12	**teeth, ears**
Harlington (Bedfordshire)	[tiːf]
Llanfrechfa (Monmouthshire)	[jœs]
Concentric Circle 13	**ask, mouth**
Latterbridge (Gloucestershire)	[haks]
Netteswell (Essex)	[mæʊf]

Figure 5.5b: IVRDM1: Distribution path of putative input items from SL
Wearhead (Northern Region)

was from all over England. This was not the case however, as will be seen from the presentation of the three remaining regions.

A smaller area of distribution than that noticed from SL Wearhead in the north of England, is seen when we move outwards from SL Canewdon in the east of England. Take a look at this distribution in IVDM2 (Figure 5.6a).

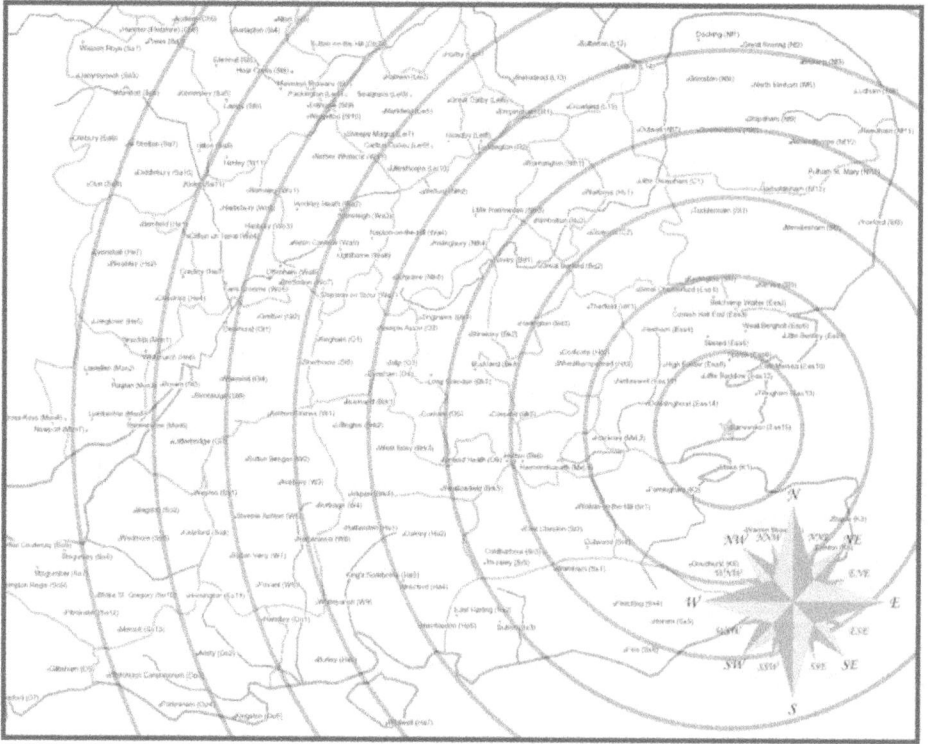

Figure 5.6a: IVDM2: Distribution of remaining putative input items from SL Canewdon (East and East Anglia region)

IVDM2 (5.6a) presents a more concentrated distribution of SED45 putative input forms, from SL Canewdon, than that observed for SL Wearhead in the north. The radius of this distribution is 216 km (8 cm), which makes it 135 km (5 cm) smaller than the distribution from SL Wearhead. This distribution of the putative input forms from SL Canewdon seemed to span all localities in the east through to the west and portions of the south of England, with no requirement to include any of the localities to the north of England. However, CCAT2 (Table 5.3) told a more precise story concerning the exact nature of this distribution.

Table 5.3: CCAT2: Canewdon (Essex) $^{23}/_{45}$ (22 variants to secure)

Concentric Circle 1	**turn, hare, burn, work**
Tillingham (Essex)	[təˤːn]
Little Baddow (Essex)	[hɛə]
Tiptree (Essex)	[bəˤːn], [wəˤːk]
Concentric Circle 2	**hungry, corn, broth, more (quantity), mouth**
Doddinghurst (Essex)	[hʌŋgɹɪ]
Farningham (Kent)	[gʊtʁ], [kɔˤːn]
Netteswell (Essex)	[bɹɔːf], [mɔᵊʈ], [mæʊf]
Concentric Circle 3	**door, more**
Great Chesterford (Essex)	[wɛəɹ]
Concentric Circle 4	**wear, arse, teeth, star**
East Clandon (Surry)	[jəɹ]
Harlington (Bedfordshire)	[aˤːʂ]
Stewkley (Berkshire)	[stäˤ]
Concentric Circle 5	**yesterday, woman**
Tingewick (Berkshire)	[ɪstəʳdɪ]
Kislingbury (Northamptonshire)	[wʊmən]
Concentric Circle 6	**Hear**
Uffington (Berkshire)	[jɪəˤ]
Concentric Circle 7	**Ask**
Latterbridge (Gloucestershire)	[haks]
Concentric Circle 8	**ears, eyes**
Llanfrechfa (Monmouthshire)	[jœs], [həɹ]

This distribution of the putative input forms follows a path from the east of England, with two diversions to Framingham and East Clandon in the south, through the midlands and ends in the west of England. This is highlighted in IVRDM2 (Figure 5.6b).

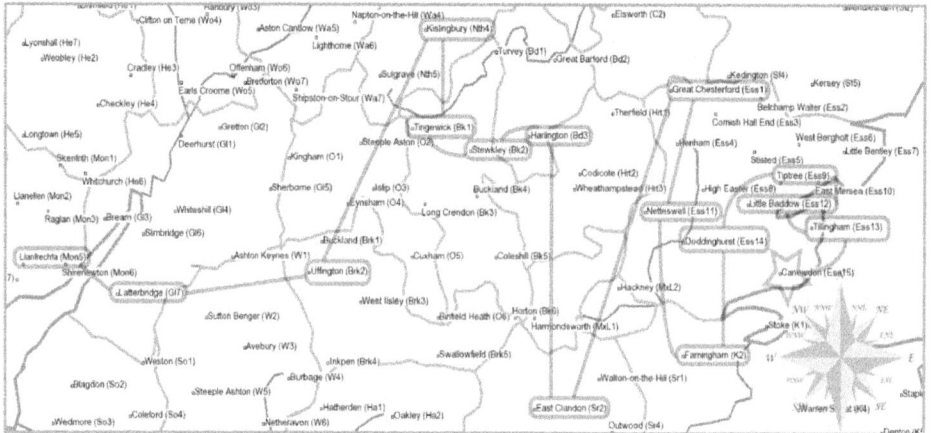

Figure 5.6b: IVRDM2: Distribution path of putative input items from SL Canewdon (East and East Anglia region)

The distribution from the west of England exhibited an even more concentrated clustering of the putative input forms than that noticed with SL Wearhead and SL Canewdon.

The radius of this distribution, from selected SL Earl's Croome, is 135 km (5 cm). This makes it 81 km (3 cm) smaller than that noticed with the distribution from the East England SL (Canewdon) and 135 km (5 cm) smaller than that noticed with the distribution from the north England SL (Wearhead).

This distribution, as seen in IVDM3 (Figure 5.7a), seems to be concentrated within the west of England with a small overlap in the east of England and a part of the western section of the south of England. Let us take a closer look at the actual locality-by-locality breakdown of the distribution.

When I transposed this information to an ivrdm, I observed a geo-linguistic distribution of input forms concentrated in the west of England with an overlap, i.e. a move to localities, in the south of England. This overlap covers the southern localities Blagdon, Wedmore and Brompton Regis (see Figure 5.7b).

In accordance with the pattern thus far, the densest distribution of the input was noticed from the final selected *Start Lect*, Blagdon, in the south of England (see the following page).

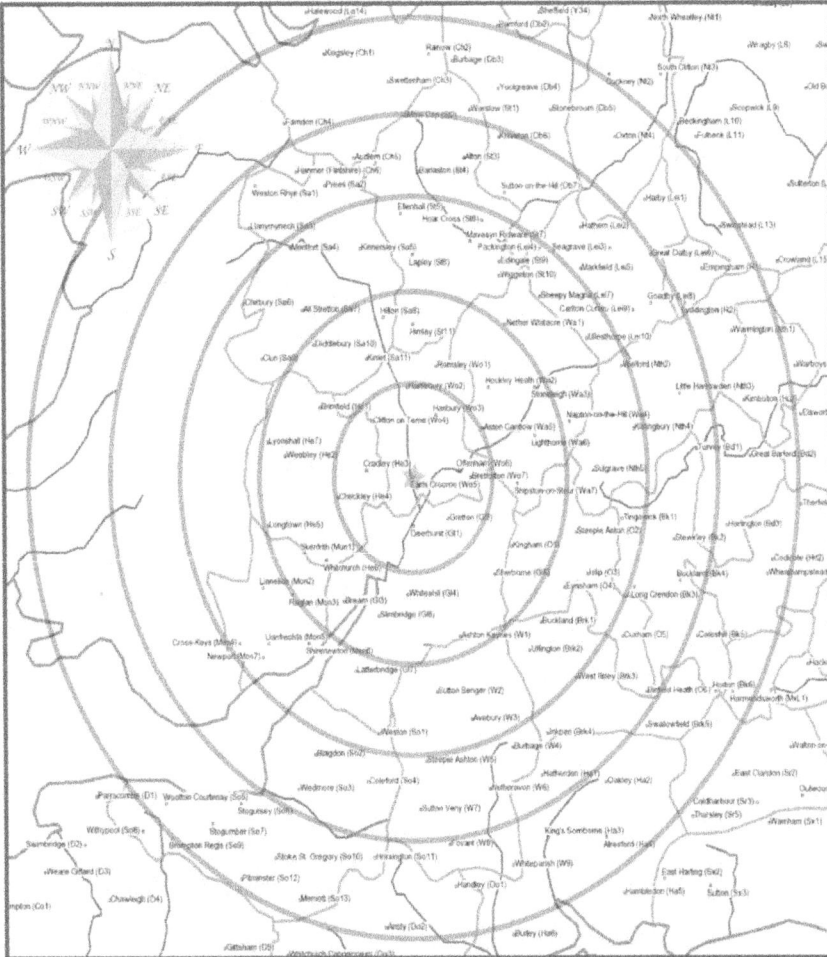

Figure 5.7a: IVDM3: Distribution of remaining putative input items from
SL Earl's Croome (West and West Midlands region)

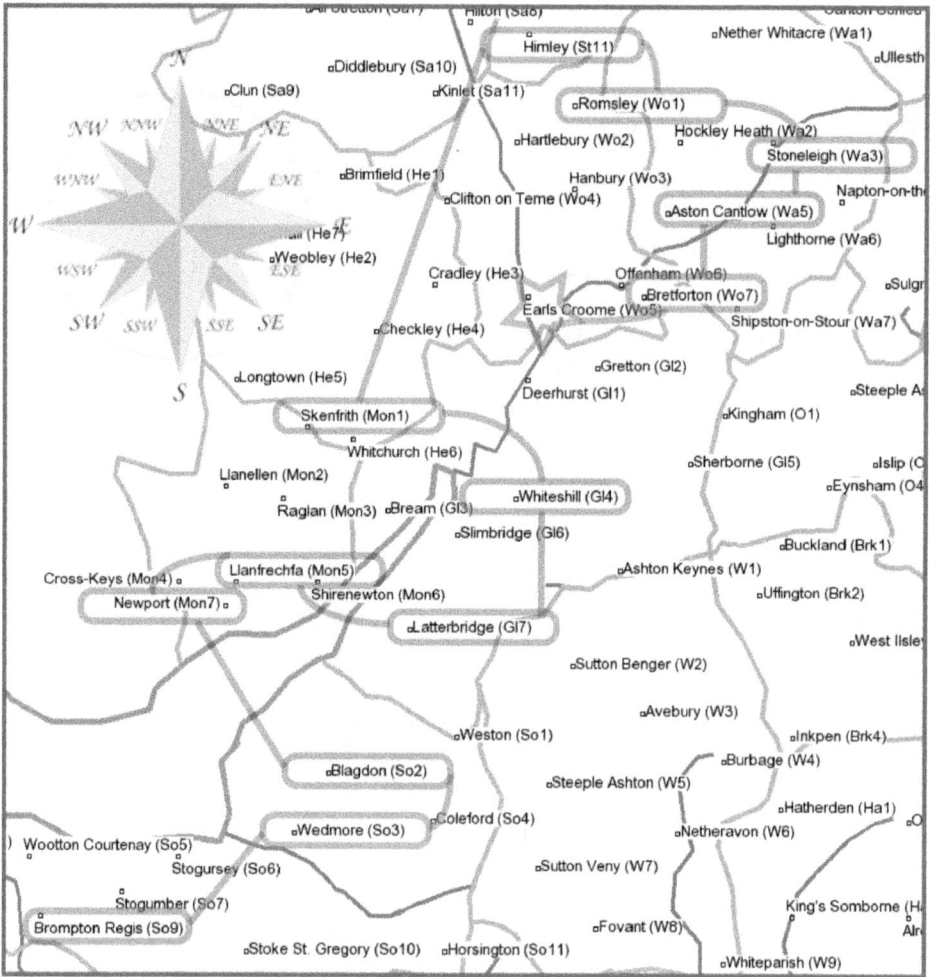

Figure 5.7b: ivrdm3: Distribution path of putative input items from SL
Earl's Croome (West and West Midlands region)

Table 5.4: CCAT3: Earl's Croome (Worcestershire) $^{22}\!/_{45}$ (23 variants to secure)

Concentric Circle 1	finger, brother, yesterday, hog, master (husband)
Bretforton (Worcestershire)	[fɪŋgə], [bɹʊðə], [ɪstəʳdɪ]
Aston Cantlow (Warwickshire)	[hɑg], [mastəˡ]
Concentric Circle 2	**hot, care, four, hear, gutter**
Stoneleigh (Warwickshire)	[hɑt]
Romsley (Worcestershire)	[keːə]
Himley (Staffordshire)	[fɔ]
Skenfrith (Monmouthshire)	[jəʳʈ]
Whiteshill (Gloucestershire)	[gʊtəʳ]
Concentric Circle 3	**ask, hurt, hand, eyes, ears, hungry, fire, house, head**
Latterbridge (Gloucestershire)	[haks]
Llanfrechfa (Monmouthshire)	[hœt], [hand], [həiz], [jœs], [haŋgɹi]
Newport (Monmouthshire)	[faɪə], [həus], [hɛd]
Concentric Circle 4	**mouth, help, broth**
Blagdon (Somersetshire)	[maʊf], [hɛlp]
Wedmore (Somersetshire)	[brɔf]
Concentric Circle 5	**teeth**
Brompton Regis (Somersetshire)	[tiːf]

The radius of the distribution from SL Blagdon is 81 km (3 cm), making this geo-linguistic distribution of the putative input forms 54 km (2 cm) smaller than the distribution from the Earl's Croome in the west of England, 135 km (5 cm) smaller than the distribution observed from Canewdon in the east of England and 270 km (10 cm) smaller than the distribution observed from SL Wearhead in the north of England. The locality-by-locality distribution of the input variants is as follows:

What CCAT4 (Table 5.5) highlights is an allocation of the putative SED45 input in the most concentrated geo-linguistic distribution. All localities in which the relevant linguistic forms are secured, fall into a geographical space characterised by an overlap of the western part of the south of England, specifically the counties of Somersetshire and Wiltshire, and, the county of Monmouthshire. Look at

Figure 5.8a: IVDM4: Distribution of remaining putative input items from SL Blagdon (Southern region)

Blagdon's ivrdm to get a visual representation of this locality-by-locality distribution of the input forms (see the following page).

The distribution presented in Figure 5.8b, represents the most concentrated distribution of the input from SL Blagdon. This distribution spans, in the west-southwest region of England, the counties Monmouthshire, Gloucestershire, Somersetshire and Wiltshire. What does all this mean? Let me summarise what these results were saying to me.

5.6 What tales do the maps tell?

Whether I began in SL Wearhead to the north of England, SL Canewdon in the east or SL Blagdon to the south, in all cases there was an observed movement towards

Table 5.5: CCAT3: Earl's Croome (Worcestershire) $^{22}/_{45}$ (23 variants to secure)

Concentric Circle 1	broth, hot, hungry, remember, gutter
Wedmore (Somersetshire)	[bɽɔːf], [hɔt], [hʌŋgɽɪ], [ɽɪmɛmbəˡ]
Coleford (Somersetshire)	[gʌtəɽ]
Concentric Circle 2	**ask, ears, finger, hurt, brother, care, hare, iron, four arse, eyes**
Horsington (Somersetshire)	[aˡːʂ]
Latterbridge (Gloucestershire)	[haks]
Newport (Monmouthshire)	[jœs], [fɪŋgə], [hœːts]
Llanfrechfa (Monmouthshire)	[bɐ̈ðə], [kɛː], [həɪ], [əɪ-ən], [fɔ]
Cross Keys (Monmouthshire)	[heːᵊ]
Concentric Circle 3	**teeth, yesterday**
Brompton Regis (Somersetshire)	[tiːf]
Burbage (Wiltshire)	[estəˡd̥eː]

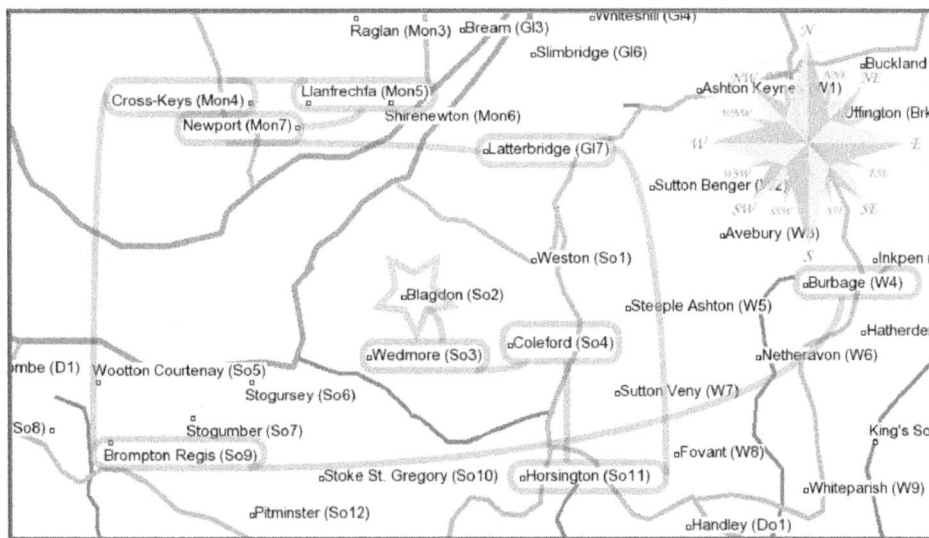

Figure 5.8b: IVRDM4: Distribution Path of Putative Input Items from SL Blagdon

the localities Llanfrechfa (Monmouthshire) and Latterbridge (Gloucestershire), in the west of England, to secure input variants for *eyes* [həɪ] and *ask* [haks], respectively (see Figure 5.9). The Sranan45 reflexes are produced with +/h/ (in this case word initial [h]) and the latter item *ask* is produced with +CCR (consonant cluster reversal), i.e. [hai] and [hakisi], respectively.

When I began in SL Earl's Croome in the west of England, there was no movement towards the north or east to secure any of the putative SED input etyma for the Sranan45. There was, however, a move to the south of England, more specifically in a south-western direction to the county of Somersetshire. The reverse was also true, i.e. when I started in the south of England, from SL Blagdon, which is situated within the western end of the southern region, there was a move towards the west of England but never to the east or towards the northern region. It is clear from this that the western end of the south of England and the west of England share a special geo-linguistic relationship.

The geo-linguistic distribution of the putative SED45 input from Earl's Croome in the west and the distribution from Blagdon in the south comprise of approximately the same localities, i.e. Wedmore, Latterbridge, Llanfrechfa, Newport and Brompton Regis. Added to this, is the fact that the geo-linguistic distribution from SL Earl's Croome also includes Blagdon.

The most densely concentrated geo-linguistic distribution of the SED45 input etyma was observed in an area characterised by an overlap of Orton's west and West Midlands and south England regions, specifically the western section of the south. This area, which I refer to as the West Southwest (WSW), comprises of counties: Somersetshire, Monmouthshire, Gloucestershire and Wiltshire. The description WSW is relevant because the geo-linguistic distribution of the putative SED input for the Sranan45 was observed halfway between Orton's West and West Midlands region and the western portion of Orton's Southern England region. At the centre of this distribution is Blagdon, which like Wedmore, Coleford, Horsington, and Brampton Regis is situated within the WSW county of Somersetshire. I therefore referred to this geo-linguistic cluster of counties, i.e. Somersetshire, together with Wiltshire, Monmouthshire and Gloucestershire as the West Southwest 4, hereafter WSW4.

I, at this point, revisited the results of the statistical analysis presented in Chapter 4 to compare these results with what I had come to know thus far from the geo-linguistic feature mapping. The following was apparent to me:

First, Blagdon's status as the most statistically significant core input dialect of origin for the Sranan45 was corroborated by the results of the geo-linguistic mapping. It is the SL at the core of the densest geo-linguistic concentration of input

Figure 5.9: North, West, East: Where three paths of geo-linguistic distribution converge

etyma. Second, Blagdon's 40% ($^{18}/_{45}$) non-corresponding putative SED45 input et-yma were found within the dense concentration of localities situated within the wsw4 cluster of localities.

Given that there was no need to venture out of the wsw4 to secure any of the putative input forms, this strongly suggested that the origin of the Sranan45 was neither from 'All-over England', nor was it from a single one of Orton et al.'s four broad regions, i.e. northern, east and East Anglia, west and West Midlands or southern England (Orton et al. 1962–71). The area of origin for the Sranan45 input etyma was in fact observed within a small geographic space in England. Based on the linguistic feature mapping this small geographic space was found to be situated between the southern portion of the west of England and the western portion of the south of England. The input localities in this small geographic area were observable in four counties that border each other. These are Monmouth-shire, Gloucestershire, Wiltshire and Somersetshire; the four counties which to-gether constitute the wsw4.

Furthermore, given the significance of the west of England, to which we must travel irrespective of SL, I was presented with another region of input that was not pinpointed by the statistical component of the methodological tool. Although no locality of statistical significance was observed in this region, it was nonethe-less a region to which movement must take place to secure the items *ask* and *eyes*, whose lexical and phonetic shapes are peculiar to that region.

In addition, there was no geo-linguistic corroboration for the east England in-put localities presented in Table 5.1. One might want to argue that choice of one of the other two potential SLs, i.e. Doddinghurst or East Mersea, over SL Canew-don, might have resulted in a more concentrated geo-linguistic distribution of the input etyma for the Sranan45. This argument can be dispelled based on the fact that whichever of the two (both of which, like Canewdon, are situated in Essex) is taken as the SL, there would still be a need to venture across East An-glia through the West Midlands to localities Llanfrechfa and Latterbridge in the west of England, to secure the two items peculiar to those localities, i.e. *ears* with word initial palatal [j] and no PVR, and *ask* with word-initial phonemic /h/ and consonant cluster reversal, /sk/→[ks].

How then, could the statistical significance of the East England lects be ex-plained? If it was only linguistic feature mapping that was done and no statisti-cal analysis then the three east and East Anglia lects would not have been pin-pointed (see Chapter 7). Added to this was one other loose end that needed to be addressed. As discussed in Chapter 4, three other localities to the south of England (see Table 5.1), presented themselves as being of near comparable statis-tical significance with Blagdon. These are: Whitwell i.o.w. in Hampshire County, with a .0078 'not by chance' probability of being the input lect, and Horsington and Wedmore in Somersetshire County, both with a .0170 'not by chance' probability of being the input lects for the Sranan45. The question was, which of the three, if any, might have provided a more credible SL, at the centre of a densely concentrated south England source for the Sranan45 input variety?

These loose ends presented me with the challenge of having to explain: (1) all the 'not by chance' correspondences being the input source for the Sranan45 and (2) which of the southern England lects, i.e. Blagdon, Wedmore, Whitwell and Horsington, provided a more viable candidate for the distribution from the south of England. Addressing the first problem would involve an explanation that included all 'not by chance' localities constituting the input for the Sranan45; this is dealt with in further detail in Chapter 7.

Addressing the second problem involved trying to determine from which of the four statistically significant wsw England lects I needed to move the shortest distance outwards, in all directions, to secure the relevant SED input for the Sranan45 reflexes. I already presented the distribution of the input from Blagdon. Hereafter I discuss the results arrived at from having plotted the distribution of the remaining putative SED input forms from the three other potential cores for the South, i.e. Whitwell, Horsington and Wedmore.

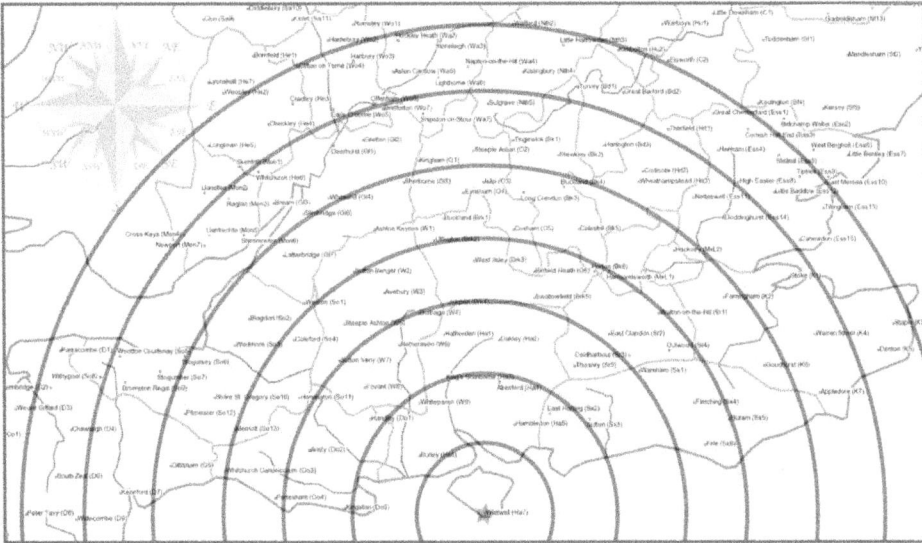

Figure 5.10: IVDM5: Distribution of putative input items from potential SL Whitwell

The radius of the geo-linguistic distribution of the putative input etyma from potential SL Whitwell is 189 km (7 cm). This makes it 108 km (4 cm) larger than Blagdon's. This distribution posed no threat to Blagdon's status of being the nucleus of the WSW4 counties, within which the input for the Sranan45 is observed. I nonetheless created Whitwell's CCAT (see CCAT5 (Table 5.6)) to see whether the geo-linguistic distribution of the putative input forms could add to, or subtract from any of the conclusions presented above.

Table 5.6: CCAT5: Whitwell (Hampshire) $^{25}/_{45}$ (20 variants to secure)

Concentric Circle 2	woman, master (husband), four, broth, mouth, teeth, hog, hungry, first
Alresford (Hampshire)	[wʊmən], [mæːstəˡ], [fɔ]
Handley (Dorset)	[bɾɔf], [məʊf], [tiːf]
Thursley (Surry)	[hɒg], [hʌŋgɹɪ], [fəst]
Concentric Circle 3	**finger**
Coldhabour (Surry)	[fɪŋgə]
Concentric Circle 4	**brother, care, fire, iron, yesterday**
Walton-on-Hill (Surry)	[bɾʌðə], [kɛ], [fɑ], [aːˀn]
Burbage (Wiltshire)	[eːstəˡdeː]
Concentric Circle 5	**ask**
Latterbridge (Gloucestershire)	[haks]
Concentric Circle 7	**ears, hurt, eye, hare**
Newport (Monmouthshire)	[jœ̈s], [hœːt]
Llanfrechfa (Monmouthshire)	[həɪ]
Cross keys (Monmouthshire)	[hɛːˀ]

Two observations were readily made about this distribution based on the localities highlighted in CCAT5 above. First, there is the anticipated movement to the west, to localities Llanfrechfa and Latterbridge, to secure the putative SED45 input etyma for *eye* and *ask*, respectively. Second, with the exception of Thursley, Coldharbour and Walton-on-Hill in the county of Surrey, which are located to the eastern end of the south of England, the geo-linguistic distribution of the putative input etyma is observed within and surrounding three of the WSW4 counties, i.e. Wiltshire, Monmouthshire and Gloucestershire. Let us now look at the other possibility, i.e. Horsington, which is situated in the county of Somersetshire.

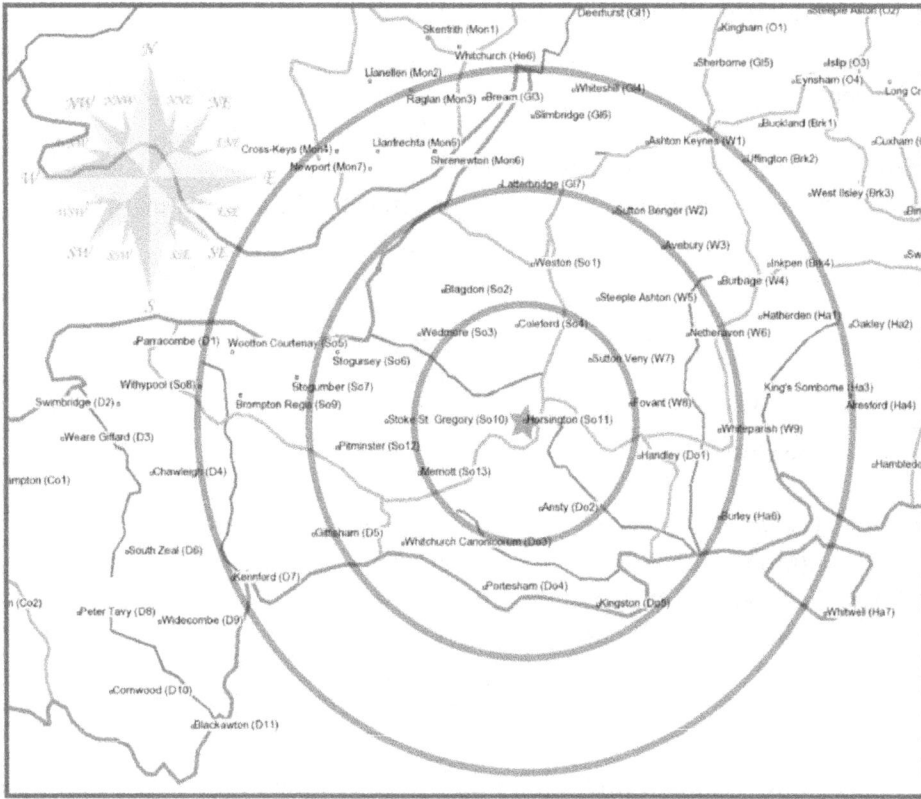

Figure 5.11a: IVDM6: Distribution of putative input items from potential
SL Horsington

The geo-linguistic distribution of the putative input from Horsington's SL posed
a challenge to my "Blagdon core" proposal. Like Blagdon the radius of its distribution is 81 km (3 cm), and its distribution seemed to encompass much of the
same localities that are found within the area that makes up the west and south
England overlap that I refer to as the WSW4. Take a look at Horsington's CCAT
(Table 5.7) to get a better idea of the type of geo-linguistic distribution that I was
presented with.

As can be seen from CCAT6 (Table 5.7) , Horsington's distribution includes
seven of the same localities found in the Blagdon distribution, inclusive of Blagdon itself. These seven localities are Wedmore and Brompton Regis in Somersetshire County, Newport, Llanfrechfa and Cross Keys in Monmouthshire County,
Latterbridge in Gloucestershire and Burbage in Wiltshire. The remaining locali-

93

Table 5.7: CCAT6: Horsington (Somersetshire) ²⁴/₄₅ (21 variant to secure)

Concentric Circle 1	**hear, broth, mouth, horse, woman, first, hog, hungry, fire**
Stoke St. Gregory (Somersetshire)	[jəᵗ:]
Handly (Dorsetshire)	[bɹɔf], [məʊf], [hasəz], [wʊmən]
Sutton Veny (Wiltshire)	[fəst], [hʌg]
Wedmore (Somersetshire)	[hɒgɹi]
Blagdon (Somersetshire)	[faɪə]
Concentric Circle 2	**ask**
Latterbridge (Gloucestershire)	[haks]
Concentric Circle 3	**four, care, iron, brother, eyes, hurt, finger, ears, hare, teeth, yesterday**
Llanfrechfa (Monmouthshire)	[fɔ], [kɛ:], [əɪ-ɪn], [bä̈ðə], [həɪz]
Newport (Monmouthshire)	[hœ:t], [fɪŋgə], [jœ̈s]
Cross Keys (Monmouthshire)	[he:ᵊ]
Brompton Regis (Somersetshire)	[ti:f]
Burbage (Wiltshire)	[estəᵗd̪e:]

ties, which are situated within one of the wsw4 counties, or in a county neighbouring the wsw4, are Stoke St. Gregory, Sutton Veny and Handley, in Somersetshire County, Wiltshire County and Dorsetshire County, respectively. Let us take a closer look at the route that has to be taken from sl Horsington to the lects that provide the remaining input forms needed to complete the Sranan45 matches (see Figure 5.11b).

Comparing IVDM4 (Figure 5.8a) (Blagdon's distribution) with IVDM6 (Figure 5.11a) (Horsington's distribution), we see where Horsington's geo-linguistic distribution of the putative input etyma poses a challenge to Blagdon's status as the core lect at the centre of the wsw4 input for the Sranan45. This presented me with the following possibilities:

1. Horsington is the core lect from which linguistic features spread outwards, prior to dialect internal changes and these features became preserved in Blagdon. The problem with this possibility was that if I was to accept it, then I would also have to accept that the reverse was also possible; i.e. that Blagdon is the core lect from which the influence had spread prior to its undergoing internal linguistic changes.

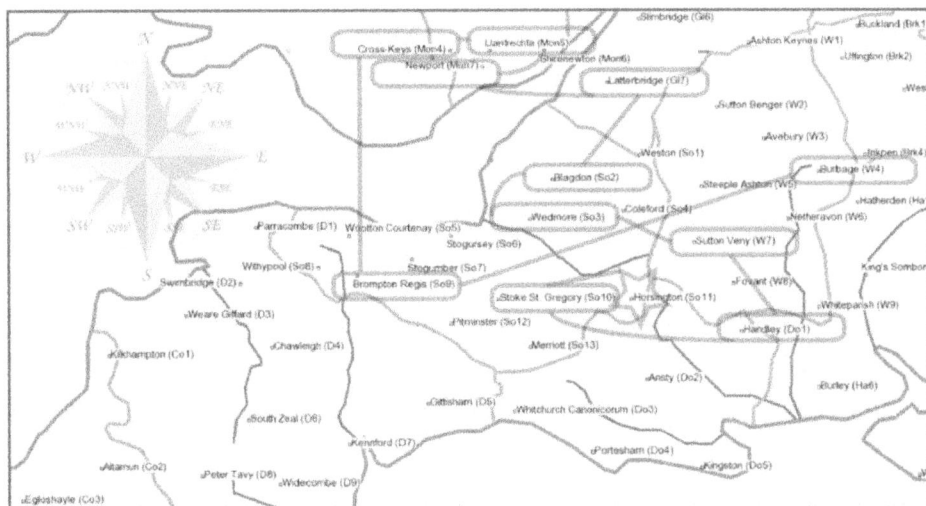

Figure 5.11b: ivrdm6: Distribution path of remaining input items from
SL Horsington

2. Blagdon is the core lect but by virtue of Horsington being in such close geographic proximity, i.e. in the same county, the linguistic feature mapping
   actually captured Blagdon's features from one of its closest geo-linguistic
   lects.

3. The input core is a Blagdon/Horsington composite.

Keeping possibilities two and three in mind, I refrained from drawing any conclusions and instead went on to look at the distribution from Wedmore, the third
and final potential core SL for the south of England (see Figure 5.12).

The geo-linguistic distribution of the putative input items from SL Wedmore
is more concentrated than noticed with Blagdon's and Horsington's. Wedmore,
which is 6.75 km (0.25 cm) away from Blagdon and 11.34 km (0.42 cm) away from
Horsington, boasts a 54 km (2 cm) radius in which all the SED45 putative input
etyma for the SRANAN45 are secured. This is 27 km (1 cm) smaller and hence more
concentrated than the Blagdon and the Horsington geo-linguistic clustering of
the input etyma. Take a closer look at the locality-by-locality distribution of these
putative Sranan45 SED input etyma.

Except for Dorsetshire, situated to the immediate south of Somersetshire and
Wiltshire, the distribution of the putative input items from SL Wedmore comprises of localities found within three of the four counties that make up the WSW4;

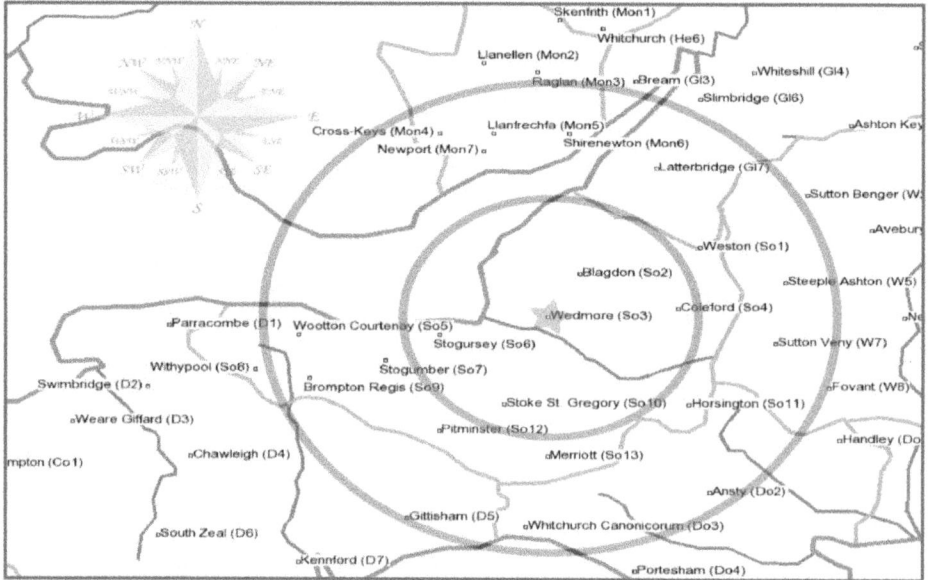

Figure 5.12: IVDM7: Distribution of putative input items from potential SL Wedmore

Table 5.8: CCAT7: Wedmore (Somersetshire) $^{24}/_{45}$ (21 variant to secure)

Concentric Circle 1	**woman, master (husband), mouth, horse, fire, hog, gutter, hear**
Blagdon (Somersetshire)	[wʊmən], [wʊmən], [mɛ:stəˡ], [maʊθ], [hɑs], [hɑg]
Coleford (Somersetshire)	[gʌtəɾ]
Concentric Circle 2	**hare, hear, arse, ask, yesterday, hurt, finger, ears, four, care, iron, brother, eyes**
Weston (Somersetshire)	[hɛːˀ], [jəˡ:]
Horsington (Somersetshire)	[aˡʂ]
Latterbridge (Gloucestershire)	[haks], [estəˡd̪e]
Newport (Monmouthshire)	[hœ:t], [fɪŋgə], [jœs]
Llanfrechfa (Monmouthshire)	[fɔ], [kɛ:], [əɪ-ɪn], [bäðə], [həɪz]
Brompton Regis (Somersetshire)	[ti:f]

96

these are Somersetshire, Monmouthshire, and Gloucestershire. In fact, this geo-linguistic area of distribution is observable at the heart of a Blagdon ~ Horsington composite distribution area. This is illustrated in Figure 5.13.

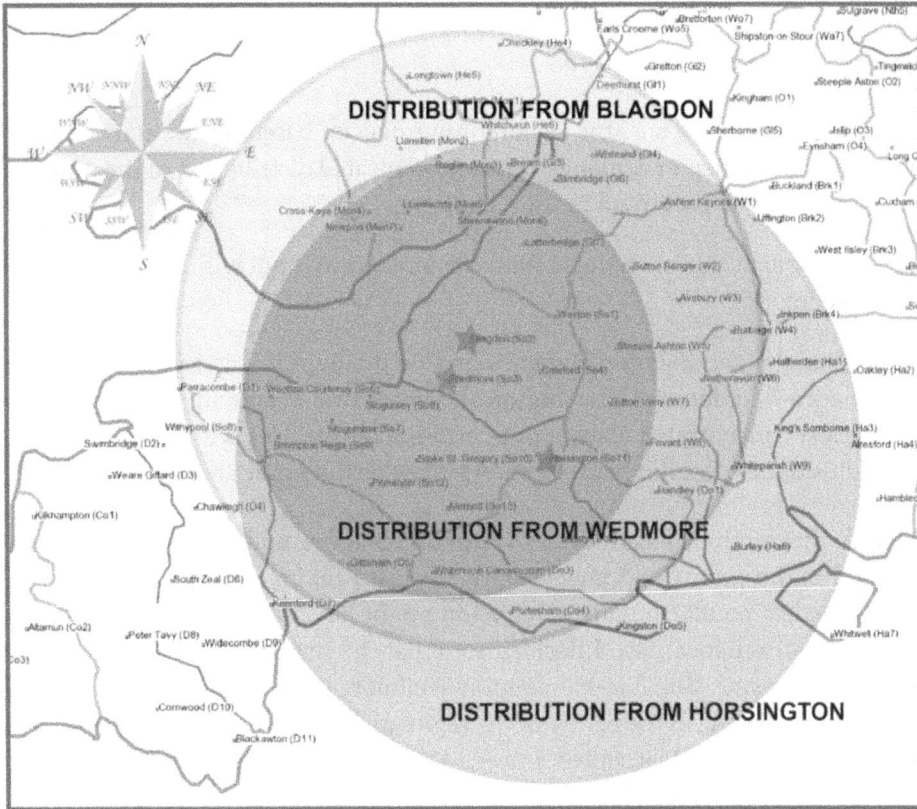

Figure 5.13: Overlapping Geo-linguistic distributions: Wedmore, Horsington and Blagdon

Figure 5.13 shows the Wedmore area (coloured green), within which we can identify the putative input items, as being a subset of the composite of the Blagdon (coloured red) and Horsington (coloured purple), areas. I had, in light of this distribution, three major contenders for the core lect of influence at the centre of the putative wsw4 regional input of origin for the Sranan45. First is Blagdon, which exhibits an 81 km (3 cm). Second is Horsington, which like Blagdon exhibits an 81 km (3 cm) long radius, geo-linguistic concentration of the putative input etyma, albeit with a three-locality difference in which some of the putative input items are secured. There is no Coleford (Somersetshire) in the geo-linguistic distribution of the putative input from potential sʟ Horsington, and there is no Handley (Dorsetshire) and Sutton Veny (Wiltshire) in the distribution from Blagdon. Third is Wedmore, with the most concentrated geo-linguistic distribution of the putative input etyma for the Sranan45; i.e. all the putative input is found within a 54km (2 cm) radius in all directions from this core lect. I contemplated for a while on whether I was to:

1. Accept Blagdon's status as core input dialect, based on the statistics presented in Chapter 4, alongside its concentrated distribution of the putative input etyma presented in this chapter.

2. Relinquish and/or share its status of core lect of input with Horsington and Wedmore.

3. Abandon the Blagdon statistics and/or the geo-linguistic similarities between Blagdon and Horsington in favour of a Wedmore core, given the 'most concentrated distribution' criteria, i.e. the area with the smallest radius of distribution being acknowledged as the input area.

Given that all three localities, i.e. Wedmore, Blagdon and Horsington, are situated within the county of Somersetshire, in close proximity to each other, I wondered whether regular linguistic diffusion might have been taking place across each of the three localities. I decided to break the impasse by selecting, at the heart of the wsw4, Blagdon-Horsington-Wedmore composite input that would serve as the core lect at the centre of the regional dialectal input for the Sranan45. However, for this to be accepted, I needed to address one other issue. This issue involved the requirement to move to the localities Llanfrechfa (Monmouthshire) and Latterbridge (Gloucestershire) irrespective of the sʟ. Located in this general area, in close proximity to three of the wsw4 counties, is Bristol, a city and port, whose importance will become more evident in Chapter 6.

Bristol, the city and port in the south of England, borders Somersetshire and Gloucestershire to its immediate southwest and northwest, respectively. To the direct north, across the Bristol Channel, is the county of Monmouthshire. I discuss in Chapter 6 the fact that this city-port played an integral role in the populating of the English New World colonies, during the period in which Suriname was settled by the English and then subsequently ceded to the Dutch, i.e. from 1650–1667.

Given the location of Bristol and its importance as a city-port during the relevant time in question, i.e. between 1650 and 1667, I asked myself the following

question: "Could it be that the localities in close proximity to Bristol, in any direction, best explained the source of influence in Sranan?" If this were true, then
I would have a possible means by which to explain the high degree of correspondence observed between the four statistically significant localities in the south
of England, i.e. Blagdon, Wedmore, Horsington and Whitwell, and the Sranan45
reflexes. Two possible scenarios came to mind. Either Bristol was the core lect of
influence from which the surrounding communities took and preserved various
linguistic features; or, the city-port was a melting pot of linguistic ingredients
coming from the surrounding farming communities. I needed to look at what
the geo-linguistic distribution of the putative input items would look like if we
began from Bristol, to see what light might have been shed on this matter (see
Figure 5.14).

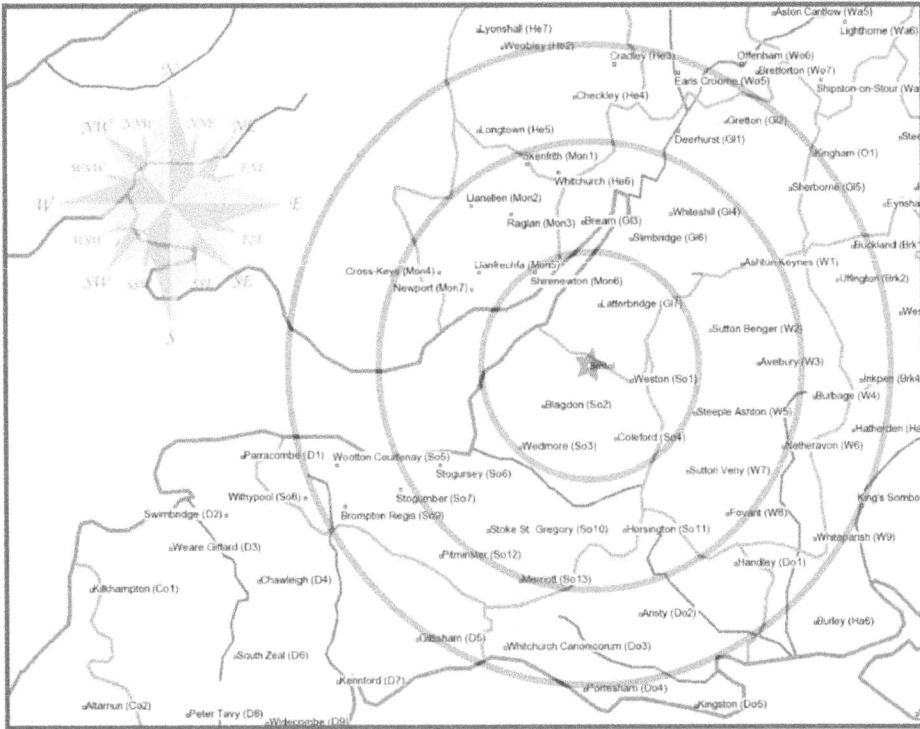

Figure 5.14: IVDM8: Distribution of putative input items from potential
SL Bristol

IVDM8 (Figure 5.14) highlights a distribution of the putative input that seems to
comprise of the same localities observed in the distributions noticed from Blag-

don, Horsington and Wedmore, inclusive of the three localities themselves; this distribution does not involve Whitwell, though it does include some portions of the Western end of the county of Hampshire. Take a look at the locality-by-locality breakdown to get a good idea of what type of distribution we are dealing with.

Table 5.9: CCAT8: Bristol ⁣$^{x}\!/_{45}$ (45 variants to secure)

Concentric Circle 1	arse, ask, yesterday, fire, hog, first, hand, head, help, house, master (husband), mouth, burn, cold, corn, curse, door, gold, hear, herring, horse, more (quantity), more, old, star, turn, woman, wear, work (noun), work (verb), gutter, broth, hungry, hot, remember
Latterbridge (Gloucestershire)	[aɹs], [haks], [ɪstəˡdɪ]
Blagdon (Somersetshire)	[faiə], [hɔg], [fɒst], [hænd], [hɛd], [hɛlp], [haʊs], [mestəˡ], [maʊf], [bəˡːn], [koʊld], [kaˡːn], [kɒs], [dɔˡ], [goʊld], [jəˡ], [haɽɪn], [hʌs], [mɔˡː], [mɔˡ], [oʊl], [staʳː], [təʳːn], [wʊmən], [wɛˡ], [wəˡk], [wəˡk]
Coleford (Somersetshire)	[gʌtəɽ]
Wedmore (Somersetshire)	[bɽɔːf], [hʊgɽi], [hɔt], [ɽɪmɛmbəˡ]
Concentric Circle 2	brother, eye, ears, four, care, hurt, iron, finger, hear
Llanfrechfa (Monmouthshire)	[bädə], [həɪ], [jǽs], [fɔ], [kɛː], [hœːt], [əɪ-ɪn]
Newport (Monmouthshire)	[fɪŋgə]
Cross Keys (Monmouthshire)	[heːˀ]
Concentric Circle 3	teeth
Handley (Dorset)	[tiːf]

Similar to the geo-linguistic distribution of the putative input from Blagdon and Horsington, Bristol boasts an 81 km (3 cm) radius in which all input etyma are secured. This provides competition for the Blagdon-Horsington-Wedmore composite input lect proposal. Barring Dorsetshire, the localities observed within the distribution of the input items from Bristol, are situated in three of the four WSW4 counties, i.e. Somersetshire, Gloucestershire and Monmouthshire. Blagdon, the locality of highest correspondence to the Sranan45 and Wedmore, the locality with the most concentrated distribution of the putative input, are found within this distribution. However, the greatest number of the Sranan45 English etyma is observed in Blagdon (see CCAT8 (Table 5.9)).

The SED did not cover urban areas and therefore excluded Bristol. Consequently, it was not possible to determine whether in the time of the SED survey, the Bristol linguistic forms could have provided a perfect match for the 45 putative input needed for the Sranan45. However, it is clear that the port and the localities within the surrounding counties, specifically those in Somersetshire and others within and around the remaining wsw4 counties, contributed significantly to the Sranan input (see Figure 5.15). This is because all relevant lexical and phonetic and idiosyncratic lexical and phonetic linguistic input forms are found within a dense wsw4 concentration of localities that are within close proximity to Bristol.

5.7 Summary of findings and the way forward

Whether I began from SL Wearhead in the north of England, or SL Canewdon in the east of England, there was need to go to localities within the wsw4 to secure various idiosyncratic items specific to that region. There was a move specifically to localities Latterbridge, Newport and Llanfrechfa, which are the only lects in which three peculiar items were observed; i.e. *ask* [haks] with word-initial [h] and +CCR /sk/ → [ks], *eye* [həɪ] with word initial [h] and *ears* [jǽs] with +Pal., respectively.

When, on the other hand, I began from the SLs Earl's Croome and Blagdon, in the west and south of England respectively, there was no need to go anywhere outside of the wsw4 to secure any of the potential input etyma for the Sranan45. This wsw4 England concentration of acceptable input etyma for the Sranan45 therefore represented strong evidence against an "all-over" England account of origin. As it concerns the issue raised regarding whether there was any denser distribution of the input than noticed from Blagdon, the answer is yes, since the distribution from Wedmore provided this denser distribution. Notwithstanding, Wedmore formed part of a composite core lect, alongside Horsington and Blagdon (all in Somersetshire county) that formed the central core of a wsw4 region of input; this region includes the counties Somersetshire, Wiltshire, Monmouthshire and Gloucester. The dialect geography tool did not, however, account for the three statistically significant East Anglian localities of Canewdon, Doddinghurst and East Mersea. I still needed to explain these three lects. These results led to two questions that the third component of my methodological tool would need to answer. The first is as follows:

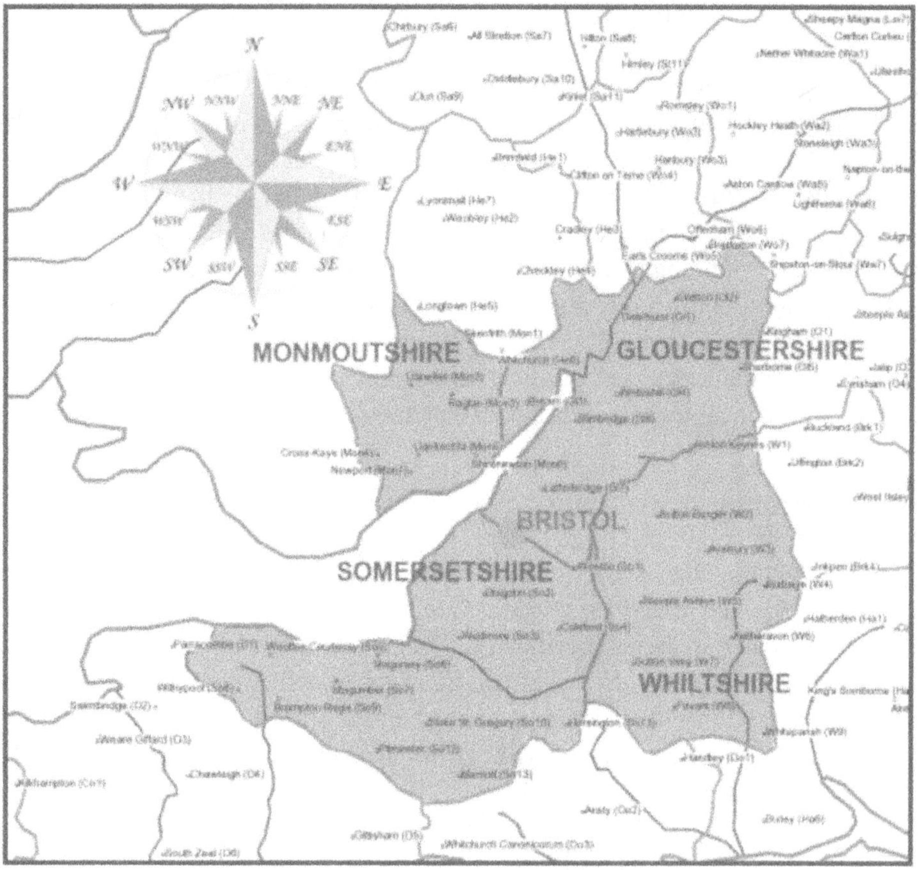

Figure 5.15: The wsw4 counties in proximity to the port of Bristol

*"Do we have historical evidence of migration from the wsw4 and its neigh-
bouring counties, going to Suriname, via Bristol and/or from any other port,
within the period 1650–1667?"*

If the answer to the above question were in the affirmative, this would represent corroboration of the results of the statistics and the linguistic geography,
thereby providing strong evidence for a wsw4 input. The second question is as
follows:

*"Do we have historical evidence of migration from any nearby port in the east
and East Anglia localities of England, going to Suriname within the period
1650–1667?"*

The answer to this question, if in the affirmative, would provide support for that part of the results of the statistical analysis that presented three statistical probable East Anglian input lects for the Sranan45. These questions and more are addressed in Chapter 6, *The Historical Complement.*

6 The historical complement

6.1 Introduction

Statistical analysis and Geo-linguistic Feature Mapping, as discussed in Chapters 4 and 5 respectively, were used to independently determine the potential source, in England, for the Sranan45 reflexes. The conclusions arrived at from having subjected the SED45~Sranan45 correspondence data to these first two components of analysis are as follows:

1. The origin of Sranan45's putative input is not from *'All-over England'*.

2. Statistically speaking, there is a possible east and East Anglia influence but the dialect geography analysis provides no corroboration for this. Nonetheless, this cannot be left unexplained.

3. Bristol, the major city-port, is most likely not the lect of influence, but this can neither be effectively proven nor disproven since the SED survey was not carried out in this urban area. However, Bristol does have an important role to play in this story, as will become clear in this chapter.

4. There is strong statistical and dialect geography confirmation for a WSW England origin; specifically a cluster of counties designated WSW4, at the nucleus of which is the influential county of Somersetshire where a core Blagdon-Horsington-Wedmore composite lect is found.

The above-restated conclusions from Chapters 4 and 5, i.e. from the Statistics and Dialect Geography components, presented me with major questions that I attempt to address in this chapter. These questions, restated here, are as follows:

1. Can we establish a chain of migration from England to Suriname, between the years 1650 and 1667?

2. Can we establish a chain of migration from England, within the same time span mentioned in (1), to the English colonies in the Caribbean and subsequently Suriname?

3. If the answer to (1) and/or (2) is in the affirmative, then what proportion of the total number of migrants to the Caribbean, specifically Suriname, is from the localities pinpointed in Chapters 4 and 5?

Before moving any further into the discussion of how these questions were addressed, there is need to provide a synopsis of the 17th century English presence in the New World and a few of the main issues that lead to their migration to the Americas. These issues are discussed under two headings – the major social issues and the major political issue.

6.1.1 The major social issues in seventeenth century England

England was, in the 17th century, a country in which many of its people endured great hardships during the reign of King Charles I, i.e. from 1625–1649 (Parker 2011: 25). The types of hardships endured under his reign eventually lead to the migration of a great number of people. Fisher et al. (1990: 145) described England, in that period, as a country in which "population pressure was gradually reducing many to poverty ..." This view is shared by Beckles (1989: 37), who suggested that it was a country on the verge of economic ruin, due to its expanding population and the scarcity of resources to support its people. This inability to provide for a rapidly growing population would eventually lead to an increase in social polarization in England. This was because "the rising demand for food brought prosperity to those who owned arable land but impoverishment to those who did not" (Amussen 2009: 3). Consequently, "Merrie England" no longer held any meaning for the working class Englishmen, because "they had no land to cultivate..." (Bridenbaugh 1968: 394).

This was not the only social issue confronting the English. According to Rogers (1889: 57), "in no period of previously recorded history was scarcity so recurrent and so prolonged," than in the 17th century. Between 1646 and 1651, England suffered through a devastating famine. But England's period of suffering did not end there; between 1658–1661, England once again succumbed to another four years of famine (Rogers 1889: 57).

England's volatile social and economic situation explained the then predominant 17th century Mercantile economic theory in England (and also France), which viewed the West Indian colonies as a demographic safety valve (Johnson 1922; Ayearst 1960; Games 2008); this Mercantile theory, remained dominant well until the 18th century, by which time the English colonies were seen as a "... zenith of prosperity ..." (MacMillan 1970: 48). Improving England's economic and social conditions therefore meant that there was need for large-scale migration, whether coerced or voluntary (Amussen 2009); to this end, by the end of the 17th century, of an estimated 700,000 British Isles (Scotland, Ireland, England, etc.) migrants going to the New World (Games 2008: 54), an estimated 350,000 of these were Englishmen "... relieving their country of the supposed burden ... of superfluous multitudes ..." by taking advantage of the promise of free land in the American mainland and Caribbean colonies (Zahedieh 2001: 402). The majority of the English migrants to the colonies, who mostly consisted of indentured servants, would not only aid in alleviating the overpopulation issue in England, but they turned out to be the biggest contributor to one of "... the most effective labor institution ... [i.e. White servitude] ... for English New World Development" (Beckles 1989: 36). White servants provided an all-important body of skilled workers and defence for the English colonies citepAmussen09.

The English arrived in the West Indies in 1624, settling first in St. Christopher, i.e. modern day St. Kitts. Settlements then appeared in Barbados in 1627 (Dunn 1973), Nevis in 1628 (Wroughton 2006), and in Antigua and Montserrat in 1632, respectively (Forsyth 1869). By the 1650s, Barbados, closely followed by St. Kitts and to a lesser extent Nevis and Montserrat, had the largest population of any settlement in the English Americas. The Leeward Islands and Antigua remained comparatively under-populated around this time, having a few Irish indentured servant occupants (Davis 1887; Galenson 2002).

6.1.2 The major political issue in seventeenth century England

Amidst the social and economic turmoil, England was also thrown into civil war between Parliament and King Charles I. The war spanned nine years, beginning in 1642 and ending on September 3, 1651 with the defeat of Charles II, at the battle of Worcester (Young & Roffe 1973). Barbados and the other English colonies were dragged into this war from 1649, when, with the execution of Charles I and Oliver Cromwell's acquired headship of the Commonwealth, they were forced to formally take the side of either supporters of the King or supporters of Parliament (Ligon 1673). This period of political tension in colonies such as Barbados intensified between 1651 and 1652, when the island colony fell under Parliamentary control (Ligon 1673; Fraser 1990).

During the years of warfare there was constant alteration between which portions of England were under the control of King or Parliament. By the autumn of 1644 for example, King Charles and his Royalist army controlled the majority of the south and west & West Midlands regions of England. By the autumn of 1645, the tables turned and Parliament gained control of the majority of the West and West Midlands territories save for a few Royalists garrisons in Chestershire,

Worcestershire and Plymouth (Gaunt 2003). The defeat of the Royalist armies was attributed to the fact that even when the Royalists were in control, there were small pockets of Parliamentary strongholds within the once Royalist controlled West and West Midlands territories (Gaunt 2003).

With the control of the west and West Midlands territories in the hands of Parliament, they, i.e. Parliament, made good use of the city port of Bristol and to this end Barbados saw a constant stream of English migrants to the island. These migrants consisted of a great number of gentry from the southern and western counties; these were captured officers of the King's Royalist army, who opted to be "Barbadosed" rather than face a life of imprisonment (Harlow 1926; Pugh & Crittall 1957; Wheeler 2002; Manning 2006).

Given the social and political issues facing England from as early as the 1630s outmigration to the English colonies, as mentioned above, was seen by many as the only option they had for a normal and prosperous life. Consequently, Barbados, the island colony to which most of the migrants went by the late 17th century, soon became overpopulated. This over-population was due, at first, to the influx of White indentured servants, and subsequently, with the rise of sugar production, by the importation of large numbers of enslaved Africans (James 1998) who gradually began to outnumber the Whites (see Campbell 1977; 1984; Campbell & Scott 1993; McCusker & Menard 1991; Galenson 2002); this is illustrated in Table 6.1 below.

Table 6.1: Population of Barbados, 1630-1690 (Sources: Campbell 1977; 1984; McCusker & Menard 1991)

Year	White	Black	Total
1630	900	100	1000
1640	13,500	500	14,000
1650	30,000	12,800	42,800
1660	26,200	27,100	53,300
1670	22,400	40,400	62,800
1680	20,500	44,900	65,200
1690	17,900	47,800	65,700

From the onset of their arrival, enslaved Africans were placed to work side-by-side in the fields with the indentured labourers who greatly outnumbered them (see Table 6.1 above) until around the late 1660s, early 1670s onwards (Davies 1974; Blackburn 1998; Galenson 2002; Elliott 2007; Bannet 2011). As the number of enslaved Africans grew, the role of the English indentured servants shifted; the indentured servants were soon charged with the task of teaching sugar production skills alongside other trades, to the Africans (Galenson 2002).

6.1.3 The English settle Suriname

Barbados, for England, was "a nursery for planting ... Surinam" (Sainsbury 1880). Lord Francis Willoughby, the then 'Governor of Barbados and the Caribee Islands' (Hotten 1874), settled Suriname in 1650. Willoughby sent Anthony Rouse to secure the mainland country on his behalf and several months later, about one hundred Whites with an unmentioned number of enslaved Africans entered Suriname (Kambel & MacKay 1999). Between 1650 and 1666, it is estimated that some 17,000 Whites migrated from Barbados (Hornsby & Hermann 2005), with over 2,000 of these persons going to Suriname (Campbell 1986).

Campbell (1986) postulated that by 1660 Suriname's population consisted of well over 1,000 persons and well over 4,000 persons by 1663, due to migration from Barbados. These 4,000 persons, according to Jacobs & Wellenreuther (2009: 44), consisted of "... 1,000 European settlers and 3,000 African slaves." By 1665, Suriname became an exceptional colony when compared to the other English colonies. Its planters consisted of practised colonists, Barbadian pioneers with their enslaved Africans and "Barbadosed" Royalist exiles, who considered Suriname an attractive colony to settle in (Harlow 1926; Pugh & Crittall 1957; Wheeler 2002; Arbell 2002; Manning 2006). The English presence in Suriname was short-lived however. At the end of the Anglo-Dutch War of 1665–1667, Suriname fell into the hands of the Dutch after seventeen years of English control and this resulted in periods of English outmigration, between 1667–1669 and between 1671–1675.

On July 31, 1667, via the peace treaty of Breda, the colony was officially ceded to the Dutch for New Amsterdam (present day New York). Given the terms of the treaty, all migration from England into Suriname ceased and the English planters on the mainland colony were granted permission to leave (Arbell 2002). Sixty-seven English planters with 412 enslaved Africans were "conveyed away by Lieut.-Gen. Willoughby" in 1668 (Sainsbury 1880: no. 1759 II); 300 English with 1,200 Negros left for Jamaica in 1669 (Sainsbury 1889; Griffiths & Griffiths 1797) and another 517 persons, Whites and enslaved Africans, left in 1671 (Sainsbury 1880).

After three years passed, on February 9, 1674 via the Treaty of Westminster, the terms agreed upon in the 1667 Treaty of Breda were reaffirmed; i.e. that English subjects were free to sell their estates and depart from Suriname. Nevertheless, the Dutch wished to retain the practised English planters because they saw no gain to be made without them. England, however, wanted them in Antigua, Montserrat and Jamaica. Consequently, on August 9, 1675, Mr Edward Cranfield, "upon His Majesty's commission and instructions of 28th March 1675," evacuated another 250 Whites and 981 of their enslaved Africans from Suriname to Jamaica (Sainsbury 1893: No. 932). The final migration occurred in 1680, when "102 persons, blacks and whites, left Suriname for Antigua" (Sainsbury & Fortescue 1889: No. 1291). After this time, only thirty-nine English are recorded as having remained in the now Dutch colony (Faber 1998; Godfrey & Godfrey 1995; Arbell 2002).

6.2 Verifying seventeenth century England origins

I was not able to find any historical documents concerning migration from England directly to Suriname, so there was no way to determine whether such movement actually occurred. What is presented hereafter was therefore predominantly constructed on historical documentation that supports the second migration scenario mentioned on page 108, i.e. 17th century migration from England to the English colonies in the Caribbean, from which there was recruitment of colonists for the settling of Suriname. As mentioned before, this was done by looking at the following:

1. The origins of the British indentured servants to Barbados and other Caribbean colonies from which Suriname is settled,

2. The origins of the English governors and big planters of Suriname,

3. The English Whites leaving the Suriname region for Jamaica in 1675.

6.2.1 Origins of the seventeenth century indentured migrants

The principal source of English migrants to the British colonies, during the 17th century, consisted of indentured servants (Esposito et al. 1982). This large body of migrants included two main groups:

1. Political prisoners; exiled Royalists of the King's army. Between 1645 and 1650 the English Civil War contributed at least 8,000 indentured servants to the West Indian colonies. This large numbers of incoming servants to the British colonies, specifically Barbados, ran concurrently with the sugar boom that was being experienced in 1640s and 1650s (Brewer & Susan 1996).

2. Despairing rural English countrymen, searching for a better life far from a socially and economically unstable England. According to Clark & Souden (1988: 167), these indentured servants who willingly left for the colonies, do not match the stereotypical "vagabonds", "rogues" and "whores" "that the prevailing mythology might lead us to believe." They were low in status, low-paid workers, who had no difficulty in reaching Bristol to arrange contracts to pay for their departure to the colonies (Clark & Souden 1988). Souden's assertion is corroborated by the fact that the records of the migrants coming to the Caribbean, from the 1630s onwards, identifies these migrants as blacksmiths, yeomen, merchants, shoemakers and farmers, etc. (see Coldham 1987; Sacks 1993).

Finding out the origin of most of these indentured servants, involved detailed scrutiny of Coldham's (1987), *The Complete Book of Emigrants 1607–1660*, which as the full title explains is *'A comprehensive listing compiled from English public records of those who took ship to the Americas for political, religious, and economic reasons; of those who were deported for vagrancy, roguery, or non-conformity; and of those who were sold to labour in the new colonies'* and the Bristol *'Register of Servants to Foreign Plantations.?'* This document, originally referred to as the *'Tolzey Book of Indentures'*, contains the systematic entries of the indentures of over 10,000 English migrants, leaving from the port of Bristol, between 1654 and 1686, when the trade in indentured servants had reached its height (Currer–Briggs 1982; Morgan 1993).

6.2.1.1 Origins of the seventeenth century England migrants: Wave 1

The first wave of migration out of England occurred under the reign of King Charles I, i.e. 1625–1649. The types of social hardships endured under his reign resulted in "... 30,000 indentured servants [going] ..." to the Caribbean colonies within this period alone; "... the majority of ... [these migrants] ... were from the West country, East Anglia or Ireland ..." (Parker 2011: 25–26). In the period before the Civil War, the majority of the colonists who came from East Anglia, the south of England and the west of England were from the counties of Wiltshire, Cornwall, Somerset, Devon, Suffolk, Essex, Kent, Hertfordshire and Oxfordshire (Watts 1990; Kennedy et al. 2009). Notwithstanding the number of migrants from the west and south of England respectively, according to Currer–Briggs (1982: 137), the majority of the migrants, from the mid 1620s to 1640s, was from "the south-east and East Anglia ..." and this pattern of migration remained unchanged until the English Civil War in the 1640s (see §6.2.1.1.1).

The East Anglian emigrants were, according to Thomas & Wood (1999), better educated and more urbanized than most of their western and southern countrymen; most of them, though not all, were educated religious Puritans. This was because in the years prior to the Civil War, East Anglia had developed into a highly urbanized and religious section of England with its "own culture, ... [and] ... speech ... [which made the]... East Anglians more like each other than the rest of Britain" (Thomas & Wood 1999: 18). Although a large contingent of the East Anglian migrants, and other emigrants leaving from the London region went to Virginia and New England, approximately a fifth of the migrants who left from London in the 1630s headed for Barbados (Parker 2011). There, a number of East Anglians, and possibly a few wealthy westerners and southerners who had already bought or leased land, became the middle strata in the British colonies Thomas & Wood (1999). Also, most of the indentured servants "... who were at first classified merely as "husbandmen" ..." were in fact accompanying the persons to whom they were indentured (Watts 1990: 150).

What this told me was that there were two major groups of Whites coming in this period. There were free Whites, the majority of whom were most likely East Anglian, who became major tobacco or cotton farmers in this period, or blacksmiths and shoemakers etc., and an indentured servant majority, who migrated from within East Anglia, supplemented by large numbers from the west and the south of England, respectively (Watts 1990; Parker 2011).

6.2.1.1.1 Migration from the port of London

According to Menard (2006) and Parker (2011), approximately a fifth (20%) of the emigrants who left from London in the 1630s headed for Barbados. Of this 20% of emigrants, Currer–Briggs (1982) suggested that the majority were of East Anglian origin. Upon analysis of the indentured servants migration records collected and compiled by Coldham (1992) in *The Complete Book of Emigrants 1607–1660*, I found that I could not determine whether the majority of the London emigrants, going to the British colonies in the 1630s–1640s, were from East Anglia. This is because in numerous cases emigrants' places of origin were not provided. In 1635 for example, of the 3,190 people recorded as having left for the colonies (Menard 2006) only a few had their places of origin recorded. Table 6.2 is a presentation of my best reconstruction of a sample of the emigrants, with places of origin listed, recorded as having gone to St. Kitts and Barbados between the 1630s and 1640s.

The emigrants going to St. Kitts are important for two reasons; first, although Suriname was settled, specifically from Barbados, it was also settled, to a lesser extent, by St. Kitts (Sainsbury 1860), and second, there was constant movement between St. Kitts and Barbados in the 1630s and 1640s. One reason for this was that Barbados was attractive, to indentured servants in particular, because more opportunities awaited the emigrants to this colony (Menard 2006). For example, "servants who fulfilled their period of indenture in Barbados, in the 1630s, were more likely to become landowners after the sugar boom" (Menard 2006: 25).

Table 6.2: Migrants, with places of origins listed, going to Barbados and St. Kitts between the 1630s and 1640s

County	St. Kitts	Barbados	Totals
Devon	71	26	97
Cornwall	38	2	40
Hampshire	–	31	31
Oxford	4	6	10
London	2	4	6
Dorset	–	3	3
Ireland	2	1	3
Sussex	–	2	2
Berkshire	–	2	2
Kent	–	2	2
Hertfordshire	–	2	2
Somerset	–	1	1
Leicestershire	1	–	1
Glasgow	–	1	1
Surrey	–	1	1
Bedfordshire	–	1	1
Staffordshire	–	1	1
Cheshire	–	1	1
Yorkshire	–	1	1

What Table 6.2 highlights is the fact that in this early period of migration, i.e. the 1630s to 1640s, the majority of the migrants, with places of origin listed, seemed to have been predominantly coming from the south-western part of England, specifically the counties of Devon, Cornwall and Hampshire. These counties are in close proximity to the wsw4 counties discussed in the Chapter 4. I was therefore getting migrants from close to the "right places", i.e. localities within and surrounding the wsw4 region; I was also getting migrants, though in no great numbers, from within and surrounding the east and East Anglia England region, specifically from Bedfordshire, Hertfordshire, London, and Kent, going to Barbados and St. Kitts, the colonies from which Suriname was settled. The next step was to look at the migration patterns for the 1650s up until 1667; this being the period in which Suriname was settled and subsequently lost to the Dutch.

6.2.1.1.2 Origins of the seventeenth century England migrants: Wave 2

Beckles (1989) and Sacks (1993) suggest that Bristol was the main source of indentured labour to the British colonies in the second half of the 17th century. This is due to the fact that one of the effects of the English Civil War (1642–1651) was "... the ending of London's monopoly on trade and the growth of Bristol as a port of entry for both tobacco and sugar" (Currer–Briggs 1982: 137). Currer–Briggs (1982) pointed to the fact that this change from the port of London to the port of Bristol resulted in Bristol's normal trading routes being significantly altered. Bristol's original trading route was to Newfoundland, then to France, Spain, the Mediterranean and then back to Bristol. This was switched to a south-westward trading route, which spanned the coast of North Africa, the Lesser Antilles, the Chesapeake, back to Bristol (Currer–Briggs 1982).

This shift in the monopoly on trade from London to Bristol not only affected trading routes but also the recruiting grounds for emigrants; the recruitment grounds changed from the south-east of England to "... the Severn Valley ... [which is the rural part of the West Midlands, including Gloucestershire, Shropshire and Worcestershire] ... South Wales ... Whiltshire, Somerset and Dorset lying within a radius of fifty miles from Bristol" (Currer–Briggs 1982: 138). In the years between 1654 and 1685, Bristol supplied the British colonies in North America and the Caribbean with large numbers of indentured servants from the above-mentioned areas.

Bristol's well-kept systematic records of the servant trade from 1654–1684 (Beckles 1989) highlight the fact that Barbados alone absorbed more indentured servants from this port than any other English colony (Beckles 1989) within this period. One possible explanation is the fact that "... there was simply ... [an] ... insufficient ... [number of] ... Africans... [being transported] ... to Barbados in the 1640s and 1650s ..." (Morgan 2011: 379). This shortage of African labour is illustrated in Table 6.1. For this reason, even from the onset of Barbados' sugar boom in 1645 (Elias & Elias 2010), indentured servant labour constituted the foundation of the early British Caribbean economy (Morgan 2011). As mentioned before, these servants, upon arrival in the Barbados, were immediately put to work in the fields, alongside the enslaved Africans who had slowly began to arrive in the colony from the early 1640s (Brewer & Susan 1996; Galenson 2002; Amussen 2009). What eventually led to the total shift to an all-African labour force was the growing demand, between the 1640s and 1660s, for more hands to cultivate the land for sugar production. This was a demand that the supply of indentured servants could no longer effectively satisfy (Morgan 2011).

Bristol's monopoly on trade seemed to have lasted well into the late 17th century before we again hear about London and one other port, i.e. the port of Middlesex. The Middlesex port registers contain records for the period 1682–1685 and the London port registers for the year 1682 and the period 1718–1759 (VCDHb). I was therefore unable, given the lack of historical data, to determine whether migration took place from these two ports during the period in which Suriname was settled and subsequently ceded to the Dutch, i.e. between 1650 and 1667. In fact, the only record of migration from any area near these ports, close enough to the period of interest, i.e. 1650–1667, was in the 1630s, most notably 1635, eight years after the English settled Barbados. In that year 3,190 people are recorded as having left for the colonies, with 641 (20.1%) of these persons going to Barbados (Menard 2006). Unfortunately, as discussed in §6.2.1.1 above, the localities of origin in England of these migrants were not always provided. Let me therefore move into the discussion of the *Bristol Register of Servants sent to Foreign Plantations*, and the conclusions I arrived at concerning the composition of the indentured labour arriving in the colonies, some of whom would have eventually migrated to Suriname, mainly from Barbados, which was "a nursery for planting …" the mainland colony (Sainsbury 1880: no. 130).

6.2.1.1.3 Migration from the port of Bristol

The Bristol Register provided, in a number of cases, the geographic origins of servants, their occupations, destinations, transport ships, date of indentures, their genders and the names and occupations of their agents. The lists of origin were as follows:

- 54 counties of origin, 39 across England and 15 across Wales.

- 36 places of origin outside of England and Wales; i.e. France, Jamaica and Ireland.

- 133 cases of unknown places of origin, i.e. the indentured servants' counties could not be determined from the information given (VCDH)

Suriname was not among the destinations listed; I did, however, find records of movement to those colonies, specifically Barbados, from which Suriname was settled. Between 1654 and 1666, the years before Suriname fell to the Dutch, 6,007 indentured servants were recorded in the Bristol Register as having gone to the English colonies in the Caribbean and North America. 1,976 of these indentured servants had their places of origin recorded; 1,215 (61.49%) were recorded as having gone to Barbados, 659 (33.35%) to Virginia, 79 (4.00%) to Nevis and 23 (1.67%) to St. Kitts.

Suriname was settled, specifically from Barbados and to a lesser extent, Nevis and St. Kitts (Sainsbury 1860; Kambel & MacKay 1999; Whitehead 1996). Therefore, of the 1,976 above-mentioned indentured servant migrants, 1,317 (66.65%) of them went to Caribbean destinations from which Suriname was settled. Table 6.3 (following page) is a presentation of what number of these 1,317 migrants were recorded as coming from the different counties listed in the Bristol Register.

Table 6.3: Migrants, with places of origin listed, going to the Caribbean colonies from which Suriname was settled

| Counties | Place of origin | | | |
	Barbados	Nevis	St. Kitts	Totals
Somersetshire	194	8	1	203
Gloucestershire	139	6	2	147
Bristol	133	6	6	145
Monmouthshire	120	1	5	126
Wiltshire	110	7	–	117
Glamorganshire	71	4	–	75
Herefordshire	66	14	1	81
Devonshire	38	2	–	40
London	33	4	1	38
Worcestershire	28	2	2	32
Shropshire	28	4	1	33
Carmarthenshire	27	1	–	28
Pembrokeshire	25	3	–	28
Dorsetshire	23	4	–	27
Brecknock	17	1	–	18
Ireland	17	–	–	17
Cornwall	14	1	–	14
Cambridgeshire	13	2	–	15

Counties	Place of origin			
	Barbados	Nevis	St. Kitts	Totals
Hampshire	11	–	1	12
Staffordshire	9	2	–	11
Oxford	9	–	–	9
Middlesex	8	1	–	9
Kent	7	1	–	8
Northamptonshire	7	–	–	7
Montgomery	6	–	–	11
Derbyshire	6	–	–	6
Berkshire	5	1	–	6
Norfolk	5	–	–	5
Buckinghamshire	5	–	1	6
Breconshire	5	–	–	5
Cheshire	5	1	1	7
Lancashire	4	1	–	5
Yorkshire	4	–	–	4
Warwickshire	4	–	–	4
Lincolnshire	4	–	–	4
Essex	4	–	–	4
Leicestershire	2	1	1	4
Suffolk	2	–	–	2
Sussex	2	–	–	2
Surrey	1	1	–	2
Cumberland	1	–	–	1
Scotland	1	–	–	1
Huntingdonshire	1	–	–	1
France	1	–	–	1
Totals	**1215**	**79**	**23**	**1317**

The information presented in Table 6.3 above, is revisited in §6.3: *The tales that history tells*, which is a presentation of how the historical data matches up to the results of the statistical analysis and the linguistic feature mapping discussed in Chapters 4 and 5. The following discussion therefore concentrates on the two remaining types of historical data that were looked at in this research. These are related to the origins of the owners, governors, principal planters, etc. of Suriname and the origins of the persons recorded as having migrated from Suriname after it cession to the Dutch.

6.2.2 Origins of owners, governors and principal planters

Suriname, during the period of its being an English colony, i.e. 1650–1667, had two co-owners: Francis Willoughby and Lawrence Hyde and two Governors: Anthony Rouse and William Byam, prior to its cession to the Dutch in 1667. Suriname, by a charter of Charles II dated June 2, 1662, was equally divided between the two co-owners, Francis Willoughby and Lawrence Hyde, "... and their descendants forever ..." (Sainsbury 1880: no. 451, Griffiths & Griffiths 1797: 429).

Lawrence Hyde, who was the second son of the Earl of Clarendon (Griffiths & Griffiths 1797), was most likely an absentee owner. No historical data could be found concerning a possible visit to his properties in Suriname. Nevertheless, given the efforts of Willoughby and himself, three years after their being granted the mainland colony, "... 40 plantations of sugar and many more of tobacco had been settled ..." (Griffiths & Griffiths 1797: 429) Understandably, Hyde's life in England might not have been the most accommodating to travelling for months outside of England; he was the Member of Parliament for Cornwall (Newport) in 1660 and subsequently for Oxford from 1661 to 1679; he was also Master of Robes between 1662 and 1675 (Kippis 1757). These are but a few of the positions that he held until his death in 1711. Hyde, as with the rest of his family, originated in Wiltshire and the family also had lands in Hampshire (Jones 1862; Duke 1983).

Francis Lord Willoughby, hailed from Parham in West Suffolk (Burke 1838). In the 1650s he was Governor of Barbados (Kaufman & Macpherson 2005) and by order of King Charles, he was made Lieutenant-General and Chief Governor of St. Kitts, Nevis, Montserrat, Antigua, and several islands of the province of Caroline in 1660 (Sainsbury 1860); this gave him the title Governor of Barbados and the Caribbe Islands. There he was charged with the undertaking of the governance of those islands, either by himself or by appointment of some other Governor, who was in favour of the King (Sainsbury 1860). Willoughby, in 1650 sent Major Anthony Rouse, the man who would become Suriname's first governor, to secure and settle the mainland colony. Willoughby would eventually die in a violent hurricane while on his way to St. Kitts in 1666 (Pepys & Braybrooke 1848).

The origin of Suriname's first governor is a mystery. Not much is known about Major Anthony Rouse's origin in England. What is known about Rouse is that he was an extreme Royalist and established Barbadian planter who was sent by Willoughby, in 1650, "... with 300 people of the English Nacion ..." to settle Suriname. He was thereafter the colony's first governor from 1651–1654 (Bridenbaugh & Bridenbaugh 1972: 198, Heywood & Thornton 2007: 262). Trying to determine his England roots was difficult because though it was common practice for planters to regularly travel back and forth to England, "Rouse seemed quite settled in Barbados and Surinam" (Roper & Van Ruymbeke 2007) and I could therefore find no historical data concerning Major Rouse possibly travelling between England and the colonies.

According to Roper & Van Ruymbeke (2007: 195–197), there were "at least three contemporaneous Anthony Rouses." The first was the "nephew of Francis Rouse, the parliamentary de factoist who would become Speaker of Barebone's Parliament" (Roper & Van Ruymbeke 2007: 195). The second Rouse, who was a co-clerk of the Pipe in the service of Charles I, was of an older generation and could therefore not be the Rouse of Suriname (Roper & Van Ruymbeke 2007). The third Anthony Rouse, who had established plantations in both Barbados and in Suriname(Roper & Van Ruymbeke 2007), might well have been a grandson of Sir Anthony Rouse (RHS 1924). Sir Anthony Rouse originated from Edmerston, Devon (Burke 1838). In fact, in looking at the places of origin of the Rouse lineage, the counties Devonshire and Cornwall were consistently highlighted (Burke 1838). Given an inability to determine, with any degree of certainty, a Devonshire or Cornwall origin for Rouse, this govorner's place of origin was taken as Devonshire/Cornwall, which means that he, as with Suriname's second govorner, William Byam, came from Southwest England.

Unlike his predecessor, whose specific place of origin is a mystery, the origin of Suriname's second governor was much easier to find out. William Byam, Suriname's governor from 1654 to 1667, came from the village and civil parish of Luccome in Somersetshire (Paravisini–Gebert 1996). He, Byam, was one of the King's Royalist officers, exiled to Barbados during the Civil War in England (Paravisini–Gebert 1996).

The importance of knowing the origins of these men and by extension their families had to do with the fact that it was common practice for governors, planters and/or their agents to recruit from their shires, villages, etc., persons wishing to work as indentured servants in the colonies (Bridenbaugh 1968; Beckles 1989; Menard 2006). This was important for me to know because it meant that there was a possibility that Willoughby, Rouse and Byam, might have taken with them from Barbados, servants who might have been indentured to them, servants whose places of origin might have also possibly been the same as the owner and two governors of Suriname. In the case of Lawrence Hyde, agents working on his behalf might have also recruited indentured servants from within around the Devonshire. All this is, of course, speculation since I was unable to secure any evidence to prove whether this was indeed the case.

6.2.3 Migration from Suriname

In early 1675, English ships - Hercules, America and The Henry and Sarah, transported 1,231 persons from Suriname to Jamaica (Sainsbury 1893: No. 675 vii; 677i). Of the passengers listed as having gone on this voyage, a search of the Bristol Register turned up ten matches for names of people transported to the Barbados to 1666. These are Ann Matthews, William Smith, James Barker, John Phillips, William Slade, Thomas Cotton, John Morris, Edward Foster, John Horne and William Smith, with their places of origin recorded as Herefordshire, Wiltshire, Gloucestershire, Monmouth, Devon, Dorset, Somerset, Shropshire and Norfolk, respectively. Despite an inability to establish a direct England to Suriname link, I was getting ten names of people, matching ten names in the Bristol Register, going to Jamaica from Suriname.

Unfortunately, a match between an entry in the list of persons going to Jamaican from Suriname and an entry in the Bristol Registers of Servants to the English colonies, in this case specifically Barbados, does not necessarily mean that we are dealing with the same migrant in both cases. There was no way to therefore determine whether these were the same persons. Nevertheless, whether or not these ten persons were the same persons listed in the Bristol Registers, I was presented with evidence that people from the wsw4and east and East Anglia regions, were in Suriname, prior to its cession to the Dutch. This, for me, represented reinforcement of the Bristol records and the notion that indentured servants with the right linguistic "stuff", that would have shaped the input for the Sranan45 went from Barbados to Surinam.

6.3 The tales that history tells

The results of the statistical analysis and linguistic feature mapping discussed in Chapters 4 and 5, presented me with statistical and dialect geography evidence for Sranan's English influence originating in the east and East Anglia (specifically in the county of Essex), and also localities within the west and West Midlands alongside the western end of the south of England – an area I dubbed the wsw4. The historical data presented thus far corroborated the results of the linguistic feature mapping, by indicating that the majority of the migrants came from within the west and south of England. There is also confirmation for the existence of the East Anglian element in Suriname, as was picked up by the statistical analysis but not the linguistic feature mapping. The best way to illustrate how the historical data corroborate the findings of the statistical analysis and the linguistic feature mapping is to indicate this, on one of my Orton-based maps (see Figure 6.1), what the historical data tell us about the counties of origin of:

- All migrants from England, from the 1630s–1640s, to the 1650s onwards, coming to Barbados and the other colonies from which Suriname was settled (see Table 6.2 and Table 6.3);

- The owners and governors of Suriname;

- The persons leaving Suriname for Jamaica after its cession to the Dutch.

Figure 6.1 above illustrates a number of things based on the combined number of migrants taken from Table 6.2 and Table 6.3. These are as follows:

1. The importance of the wsw4, inclusive of Bristol and the surrounding southwest counties, to the indentured servitude trade, was corroborated by the historical records. The records, as highlighted with the map above, suggested that the majority of the indentured servants to the colony(ies), from which Suriname was settled, were indeed from the localities within and around the area that I dubbed the wsw4. Between the years 1630 and 1667, of the 1,523 migrants that I was able to account for, 1,092 (71.7%) from areas within and around the wsw4 and Bristol; 738 (48.5%) of these migrants originated within the wsw4 and Bristol and 354 (23.2%) of them from the counties, immediately surrounding the wsw4 – Dorsetshire, Devonshire, Oxfordshire Hampshire, Herefordshire, Warwickshire, Worcestershire and Berkshire.

2. A close look at the migration pattern from within the wsw4, for the period between 1630 and 1667, showed that Somersetshire, the county in which I found the Blagdon/Horsington/Wedmore core lect (see Chapter 5) had the largest number of migrants, i.e. 27.6% ($^{204}/_{738}$), leaving from England. Somersetshire was closely followed by Gloucestershire with 19.9% ($^{147}/_{738}$) of the migrants, Bristol with 19.7% ($^{145}/_{738}$), Monmouthshire with 17.1% ($^{126}/_{738}$) and Wiltshire with 15.9% ($^{117}/_{738}$) of the migrants, respectfully.

3. When I moved one county outwards (outer counties are indicated in yellow) in all directions from each of the wsw4 counties, I found that of the 354 (23.2%) migrants from these bordering counties, Devonshire had the largest number of migrants leaving the county, i.e. 39.6% ($^{137}/_{346}$). Devonshire was followed by Herefordshire with 23.4% ($^{81}/_{346}$), Hampshire

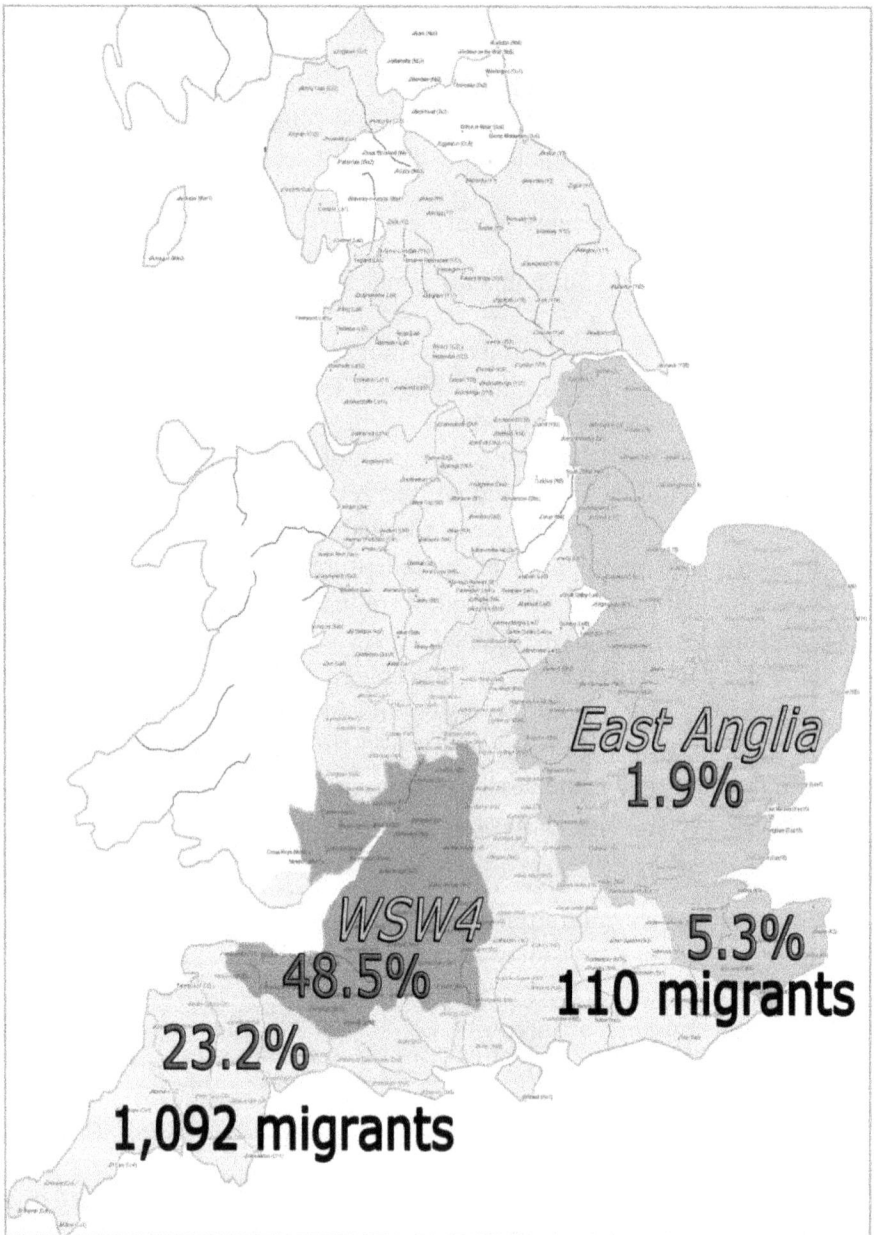

Figure 6.1: Percentage of migrants, with places of origin recorded for
1630–1667, going to the colonies from which Suriname was settled

with 12.4% ($^{43}/_{346}$), Worcestershire with 9.2% ($^{32}/_{346}$), Dorsetshire with 8.7% ($^{30}/_{346}$), Oxfordshire with 5.5% ($^{19}/_{346}$), Hampshire with 4.3% ($^{15}/_{346}$), Berkshire with 2.3% ($^{8}/_{346}$) and Warwickshire with 1.2% ($^{4}/_{346}$).

4. Of the 1,523 migrants with their places of origin recorded, I was able to identify 110 (7.2%) persons who migrated from the East Anglia region, i.e. Suffolk, Norfolk, Essex, Hertfordshire, Bedfordshire and Cambridgeshire and its immediately surrounding counties of Buckinghamshire, Northamptonshire, Kent, London, Lancashire and Middlesex. The majority of the migrants from within this area, were not recorded as coming from within the East Anglia region but from the outer east England counties (these are indicated in red) with London providing the bulk migrants for these outer counties, i.e. 54.3% ($^{44}/_{81}$).

5. Of the remaining 21.1% ($^{321}/_{1523}$) of the migrants who went to the colonies from which Suriname was settled, a substantial number of them, 30.8% ($^{99}/_{321}$), migrated from other southwestern counties; 49.8% ($^{160}/_{321}$) of them migrated from counties in Wales that bordered the west of England, i.e. Brecon, Glamorganshire, Carmarthenshire, Pembrokeshire, Brecknock and Montgomery. The remaining 19.2% ($^{62}/_{321}$) of the migrants originated from counties within the north of England or from other countries such as Ireland, Scotland and France.

I had corroboration of results from three independent components of analysis. But this only left me with pieces of a story that was waiting to be written. What were the results of statistics, linguistic feature mapping and history really saying? What did the east and East Anglian and wsw4 regions of England have in common, linguistically? What made the statistical analysis pinpoint three lects from within the east and East Anglia region, when according to the history the majority of the English influence was coming from the wsw4 England region? How could the influence of the West and West Midlands be explained? The lects in this region did not show correspondences that were statistically significant, yet they contributed three peculiar items to Sranan, i.e. *eye*, [hai] in Sranan, *ear*, [jesi] in Sranan, and *ask*, [hakisi]. The results of the three components of analysis, i.e. statistically, linguistic feature mapping, historical, therefore represented three pieces of a jigsaw puzzle. No one component told the full tale of how the English input found its way into Sranan. But, together all three painted what seemed to be a more complete picture of the input. Though more complete, this picture was nonetheless a complicated one, which led two major questions that I attempt to answer in Chapter 7. These questions were as follows:

1. How did it happen? Did individual items enter Proto-Sranan via the mouths of individual native English speakers? Or, was there a levelled colonial Barbados/Suriname variety, which provided a single set of inputs, or a mix of the two?

2. Where did it happen? Where was the colonial English input form coming from? Was it Barbados/St. Kitts or did it develop in Suriname?

7 A tale of two dialect inputs

7.1 Review

I had planned to, from the onset of this research, test the viability of a pan-dialectal versus mono-dialectal account of origin for the English dialectal influence in Sranan. I had wanted to see whether the influence originated from all over England or whether it originated from Smith's proposed southeast England (Smith 1987; 2008a). What I found, however, was more complex. The influence was neither from all over England, nor from a single dialect region, nor was it even from southeast England alone. Instead, the origin of the English lexico-phonetic influence in Sranan was from west-southwest England and southeast England. I arrived at these results via the use of a tripartite methodological tool consisting of a statistical component, a dialect geography component and a historical component.

The results of the statistical analysis of the data provided statistically significant evidence for seven potential input sources of origin for the lexical and phonetic influence in Sranan. These seven lects are Blagdon, Wedmore, Horsington, Whitwell, Doddinghurst, Canewdon and East Mersea (see Chapter 4). The results of the linguistic feature mapping corroborated the results of the statistical analysis; albeit presenting only a dense concentration of input forms in a region I dubbed the wsw4 (see Chapter 5). This region, which is inclusive of localities within the counties of Somersetshire, Monmouthshire, Wiltshire and Gloucestershire, has at its core, a composite lect of origin that included three of the seven lects identified by the statistical component of analysis. These three lects are Blagdon, Wedmore and Horsington.

The Linguistic feature mapping highlighted neither Whitwell, which is situated in the south of England, nor Canewdon, Doddinghurst and East Mersea, which are situated in the east and East Anglian county of Essex. However, the historical component of analysis, presented me with confirmation of not only the presence of a majority of 17th century migrants from the wsw4 region, but also migrants from the east and East Anglia region, alongside those counties immediately surrounding the two regions (see Map 6.1 in Chapter 6). This third level of analysis, i.e. checking the 17th century English migration history from England, triangulated the results of the statistical analysis and linguistic feature mapping by presenting a number of facts. These are as follows:

1. Prior to and during the period in which Suriname was settled by the English and subsequently lost to the Dutch, i.e. 1630–1650 and 1650–1667, the wsw4 region contributed the highest percentage of indentured servants to the English colonies, from which Suriname was settled (see Chapter 6).

2. East and East Anglian England migrants were said to have migrated to the English colonies in large numbers in the earlier period, i.e. from the 1630s to the 1640s. However, neither in the 1630s–1640s period, nor in the later 1650–1667 period did their numbers seem to outweigh those of the wsw4 migrants going to Barbados and St. Kitts, these being the two colonies from which Suriname was settled.

3. Scotsmen and Irishmen were not present in the English American colonies in any significant numbers during the period in which Suriname was an English colony. This is because migration from Ireland and Scotland did not seem to occur to any large degree, until 1716 for the Scots (see Dobson 2005) and between 1718 and 1785 for the Irish (Griffin 2001).

These results indicated to me that Smith (1987; 2008a) was not wrong in his southeast origin hypothesis; however, he may have neglected a significant west-southwest England source. As stated in Chapter 6, none of the three components of analysis, could, by itself, account for all relevant English linguistic and human presence in Suriname. The combined results, however, painted a clearer picture, though it did so without telling me the tale of how this influence came to be. In this chapter, an attempt is made to tell, based on the combined results of the three components of analysis, the "full" tale of the Sranan45's 17th century lexico-phonetic influence from England.

7.2 The tale being told

How do we explain what the results of statistics, linguistic feature mapping and history allude to? What did the east and East Anglian England and the wsw4 region of England have in common, linguistically? Writing this tale involved my attempting to answer two major questions, which consisted of smaller, more specific parts. These questions were as follows:

1. How did it happen? Did individual lexical items enter proto-Sranan (the original version of the English creole that was being created) via the mouths of individual native English speakers using the own regional dialects? Or, was there a levelled colonial Barbados/Suriname variety, which provided a single set of inputs, or was the source a combination of the two?

2. Where did it happen? Where was the colonial English input form coming from? Was it Barbados/St. Kitts or did it develop in Suriname?

7.2.1 How and where did it happen?

In order to answer the two questions presented above, there was a need to put into context what the combined results of the tripartite system of analysis were indicating. This involved determining the nature of the linguistic relatedness between the input forms from the wsw4 and southeast regions, respectively. It was theorized, based on the results of the three components of analysis, that I was dealing with a levelled and/or koineised wsw4~east and East Anglia composite lect of origin. To determine the plausibility of this theory, the degree of linguistic relatedness across the two regions was accessed (see Table 7.1).

Table 7.1: Distribution of shared and regionally peculiar SED45 input across the wsw4 and east and East Anglia regions

Lexico-phonetic shapes			
Region	Items	%	Examples
Peculiar to wsw4	15	33.3	*arse, ask, broth, corndoor, ear, eye, hearmaster, more, more, mouthstear, wear, woman*
Peculiar to East/East Anglian	6	13.3	*brother, care, fingerfour, hurt, iron*
Shared across both	24	53.3	*burn, cold, curse, fire, first, gold, gutter, hand, harehead, help, herring, hog, horse, hot, house, hungryold, remember, teeth, turn, work* (n), *work* (v), *yesterday*

The data presented in Table 7.1 highlight the following facts:

1. The Sranan45 input originated from a wsw4~east and East Anglia composite lect of origin, with the east and East Anglian influence possibly being Smith's proposed Early Modern (London) English (Smith 1987; 2008a). I arrived at this conclusion based on the fact that there is a high degree of linguistic relatedness across the two regions. Both regions had 53.3% ($^{24}/_{45}$) of the same lexico-phonetic forms needed for the Sranan45 input. Also, when I added to this number the 33.3% ($^{15}/_{45}$) and 13.3% ($^{6}/_{45}$) of the input forms that were peculiar to the wsw4 and east and East Anglia regions respectively, I secured all forty-five SED input forms for the Sranan45 reflexes.

2. The wsw4 region provided 20% ($^{9}/_{45}$) more exclusive regional input forms, i.e. 33.3% ($^{15}/_{45}$) than did the east and East Anglia region which provided 13.3% ($^{6}/_{45}$).

3. The exclusive input forms provided by the east and East Anglian region were r-less and h-full and dental fricative-less, and the exclusive input forms provided by the wsw4 region were both r-full and h-full, dental fricative-less and exhibited word-initial Palatals and consonant cluster reversal (See Chapter 4 for discussion of these features).

These results indicated to me that my theory concerning the nature of the input was plausible; i.e. that the input was some wsw4~east and East Anglia composite lect. This meant that the plot for the tale of English input for the Sranan45 was one that involved a number of possibilities. The first is that there was koineization in the colonies, i.e. either in Barbados or in Suriname, involving Smith's southeastern England, Early Modern English (Smith 1987; 2008a) and wsw4 England linguistic features. The second is that there were two linguistic codes existing alongside each other, in Barbados/Suriname, with the wsw4 migrants, due to sheer numbers providing more of the linguistic influence than the Easterners. The third possibility is that the Whites all knew, had transported to the colonies and were using, features of the 1650s Early Modern English standard that had begun to emerge in England (Smith 1987; 2008a). They would do so while mixing in peculiar features from their respective *wsw* and east and East Anglia dialects.

7.2.1.1 Working out the plot

I eventually arrived at the conclusion that the plot for the tale of input was one which, based on what the data presented in Table 7.1 was telling me, included all three of the above-mentioned possibilities. I arrived at this conclusion for the reasons discussed hereafter.

Regional dialect levelling is not wholly dependent on the physical interaction of speech communities alone. One must consider the influence of the social element. This social element was in the form of an emerging Standard English derived from southeastern England, which was the dialectal lingua franca of most persons in England (see Smith 1987; 2008a). This explained the 53.3% ($^{24}/_{45}$) shared items between the *wsw* and east and East Anglia regions. It did not, however, explain the existence of the exclusive forms from both regions. This meant that the spread, in England, of the "Standard English" forms was possibly cut short due to the years of intense out-migration; however, in the colonies, there was the development of what Siegel (1985) referred to as an "Immigrant Koine", i.e. the end result of koineization of different but related dialects following a period of colonization (see Siegel 2004). Immigrant koines

> ... result from contact between regional dialects; however, the contact takes place not in the region where the dialects originate, but in another location where large numbers of speakers of different regional dialects have migrated. Furthermore, it often becomes the primary language of the immigrant community and eventually supersedes the contributing dialects (Siegel 1985).

Like dialect levelling, koineisation involves, at first, the mixing of features from the different dialects in contact. However, levelling is characterised by "... the survival of one variant ... [such as r-full words alone] ... from a pool of competing ... [r-full and r-less] ... variants ..." (Tuten 2003: 91). This is because "dialect levelling is the process that reduces language variation" (Hinskens 2009: 313). With, koineization, however, even though there is a mixing of the features of the varieties in contact; "... the outcome of such convergence ... [of linguistic dialectal input] ... is by no means complete uniformity ..." (Bynon 1983: 193). In fact, as seen with the 33.3% ($^{15}/_{45}$) peculiar items from the wsw4 and the 13.3% ($^{6}/_{45}$) for the east and East Anglian region, regular (shared) and exceptional (residual dialectal) forms existed side-by-side in the Sranan45 colonial English input.

I accounted, in my mind, for how the input was created, but I was having a hard time determining whether the English colonial input was formed in Barbados or in Suriname. I was unsure as to how to approach this portion of the plot concerning the tale of origin of the English input in Sranan. My belief is that the creation of the Sranan input began in Barbados, i.e. the immigrant koineization process and was continuing in Suriname until this process was cut short because of the cession of Suriname to the Dutch. The only possible means by which to test this theory would be to take the English creole spoken in Barbados (hereafter Bajan) and some of the lesser varieties of English, which were spread from Barbados to the rest of the Anglophone Americas, and compare their features.

Though not the focus of this study, an attempt at a phonological comparison was made between Sranan, Bajan and some of the English varieties spoken in the Leeward Islands (see Aceto 2010; Blake 2004; Aceto 2004; Williams 2003), using two of the dominant phonetic features that presented themselves in the data (see Chapter 3). These are the ±h and ±PVR features.

The rationale was that if the koineization process was cut short in Suriname, due to the colony's cession to the Dutch, then, though I should see some similarities between say Bajan and Sranan, I should not see, for example, the rhotic and non-rhotic variation noticed with Sranan. Table 7.2 below presents a presentation of what I found out.

Table 7.2: Linguistic feature comparison: Sranan, Bajan and Leeward Island Varieties (Antigua, St. Kitts, Nevis, Montserrat, Anguilla, Barbuda)

Features	Bajan	Sranan	Leeward Islands
±PVR	*+PVR*	*±PVR*	*−PVR*
±h	*+h*	*+h*	*+h*

The data presented in Table 7.2 illustrate a phonological continuum. At the midpoint of the continuum was Sranan, whose koineization/levelling process was cut short, as illustrated by the presence of variability in rhoticity. To the right and left of Sranan are Bajan and the Leeward Islands varieties, with no variation in rhoticity, which means that the koineization/levelling process was completed in favour of Rhoticity for Bajan and non-rhoticity for the Leeward Islands varieties. This is illustrated by the fact that Bajan is rhotic and the Leeward Islands varieties are non-rhotic. For me this meant that there was a possibility that any Bajan immigrant koine was not yet fully created by the time migrants left Barbados for Suriname. Based on the above discussion the following tale of origin can be proposed for the lexico-phonetic input from England into Sranan. In pursuit of a better life and for fear of incarceration due to political affiliation during the Great Civil War, two great 17th century exoduses occurred from England. The destination of the migrants from England was the English-owned American colonies, such as Barbados and St. Kitts. These colonies represented a chance for a new life away from the social and political troubles they faced in England.

Migrants came in great numbers, specifically from within and around the wsw4 and the east and East Anglian regions of England. These migrants shared common linguistic features, but they also used linguistic forms that were peculiar to their respective regions. In Barbados, their mix of shared and peculiar linguistic forms became the colonial target language for enslaved Africans who soon began to enter the colonies. Some of the migrants now turned colonists, and the enslaved Africans, eventually left or were taken from Barbados to settle in other England-owned colonies such as Suriname and the islands of the Eastern Caribbean. For those who went to Suriname, the variability found within the colonial English that they spoke remained with the enslaved Africans who remained in the country after its cession to the Dutch.

For those migrants and enslaved Africans who went to the Leeward Islands, they eventually levelled out this variability in favour of a non-rhotic accent but for those who stayed in Barbados they levelled out the variability in favour of a rhotic one. Sranan therefore represents a linguistic fossil of the early colonial English that contributed to its development. It was Colonial English that survived in an English creole, within a social and linguistic ecology that was devoid of continued Colonial English linguistic influence, from outside of Suriname, after 1667.

7.2.2 The way forward

The cutting edge of linguistic research is to be found in the use of methodological tools such as the one used in this research, to reconstruct language history. My work could be taken as a spin-off of those works that seek to reconstruct, via mathematical procedures the spread of human languages. One such contemporary work is that of Atkinson (2011: 348), who, via statistical analysis of the "... phoneme counts derived from the Worlds Atlas of Language Structures ... [database]" was allegedly able to show that "... global phonemic diversity was shaped by a serial founder effect during the human expansion from Africa ... ".

Unlike Atkinson (2011), my research did not concentrate on attempting to reconstruct the spread of linguistic genetic features around the world. Instead, via a tripartite tool, which also used dialect geography and historical data as a means of triangulating the results of the statistical analysis, I attempted a reconstruction of the spread of English lexico-phonetic genetic features from English into a creole language spoken in Suriname. The use of this methodological tool can bear fruit if applied to all Atlantic English creoles and also the relatively understudied 'lesser-known varieties of English' (see Aceto 2004; Williams 2003; Trudgill

2002). This is because it allows us to trace the relationships across these creole languages and also to determine the origin(s) of the original lexico-phonetic stock from England for example. The use of the tool is, of course, dependent on our ability to secure the most archaic forms of our creole of interest, especially in cases where decreolization has resulted in certain English creole languages becoming more like their lexifier languages. The tool is also applicable to the stock of African lexicon in relation to creole forms coming from various African languages. Imagine being able to determine, for example, the precise Eastern Ijo dialectal region from which the Ijo words in Berbice Dutch creole originated. The future path of comparative linguistic research is clear; it is to be found in the use of mathematically-based methodologies such as the one that was fashioned and used to undertake this research.

Appendix

34. Halewood (La14)

35. Harwood (La12)

36. Marshside (La10)

37. Pilling (La6)

38. Read (La9)

39. Ribchester (La8)

40. Thistleton (La7)

41. Yealand (La3)
    Yorkshire (Y)

42. Askrigg (Y7)

43. Bedale (Y8)

44. Borrowby (Y9)

45. Burton-in-Lonsdale (Y12)

46. Carleton (Y27)

47. Cawood (Y24)

48. Dent (Y5)

49. Easingwold (Y16)

50. Ecclesfield (Y32)

51. Egton (Y4)

52. Gargrave (Y17)

53. Golcar (Y29)

54. Grassington (Y14)

55. Helmsley (Y10)

56. Heptonstall (Y21)

57. Holmbridge (Y30)

58. Horton in Ribblesdale (Y13)

59. Leeds (Y23)

60. Melsonby (Y1)

61. Muker (Y6)

62. Nafferton (Y20)

63. Newbald (Y25)

64. Pateley Bridge (Y15)

65. Rillington (Y11)

66. Sheffield (Y34)

67. Skelmanthorpe (Y31)

68. Skelton (Y3)

69. Spofforth (Y18)

70. Stokesley (Y2)

71. Thornhill (Y26)

72. Tickhill (Y33)

73. Welwick (Y28)

74. Wibsey (Y22)

75. York (Y19)

WEST AND WEST MIDLANDS
Cheshire (Ch)

76. Audlem (Ch5)

77. Farndon (Ch4)

78. Kingsley (Ch1)

79. Rainow (Ch2)

80. Swettenham (Ch3)

81. Flintshire Hanmer (Ch6)
Derbyshire (Db)

82. Bamford (Db2)

83. Burbage (Db3)

84. Charlesworth (Db1)

85. Kniveton (Db6)

86. Stonebroom (Db5)

87. Sutton on the Hill (Db7)

88. Youlgreave (Db4)
Shropshire (Sa)

89. All Stretton (Sa7)

90. Chirbury (Sa6)

91. Clun (Sa9)

92. Diddlebury (Sa10)

93. Hilton (Sa8)

94. Kinlet (Sa11)

95. Kynnersley (Sa5)

96. Llanymynech (Sa3)

97. Montford (Sa4)

98. Prees (Sa2)

99. Weston Rhyn (Sa1)
Staffordshire (St)

100. Alton (St3)

101. Barlaston(St4)

102. Edingale (St9)

103. Ellenhall (St5)

104. Himley (St11)

105. Hoar Cross (St6)

106. Lapley (St8)

107. Mavesyn Ridware (St7)

108. Mow Cop (St2)

109. Warslow(St1)

110. Wigginton (St10)
Herefordshire (He)

111. Brimfield (He1)

112. Checkley (He4)

113. Cradley (He3)

114. Longtown (He5)

115. Lyonshall (He7)

116. Weobley (He2)

117. Whitchurch (He6)
Worcestershire (Wo)

118. Bretforton (Wo7)

119. Clifton upon Teme (Wo4)

Appendix

120. Earl's Croome (Wo5)

121. Hanbury (Wo3)

122. Hartlebury (Wo2)

123. Offenham (Wo6)

124. Romsley (Wo1)
Warwickshire (Wa)

125. AstonCantlow(Wa5)

126. Hockley Heath (Wa2)

127. Lighthorne (Wa6)

128. Napton on the Hill (Wa4)

129. Nether Whitacre (Wa1)

130. Shipston-on-Stour (Wa7)

131. Stoneleigh (Wa3)
Monmouthshire (Mon)

132. Crosskeys(Mon4)

133. Llanellen (Mon2)

134. Llanfrechfa (Mon5)

135. Newport (Mon7)

EAST AND EAST ANGLIA COUNTIES
Nottinghamshire (Nt)

152. Cuckney (Nt2)

153. North Wheatley (Nt1)

154. Oxton (Nt4)

155. South Clifton (Nt3)
Lincolnshire (L)

136. Raglan (Mon3)

137. Shirenewton (Mon6)

138. Skenfrith (Mon1)
Gloucestershire (Gl)

139. Bream (Gl3)

140. Deerhurst (Gl1)

141. Gretton (Gl2)

142. Latteridge (Gl7)

143. Sherborne(Gl5)

144. Slimbridge (Gl6)

145. Whiteshill (Gl4)
Oxfordshire (O)

146. Binfield Heath (O6)

147. Cuxham (O5)

148. Eynsham (O4)

149. Islip (O3)

150. Kingham (O1)

151. Steeple Aston (O2)

156. Beckingham(L10)

157. Crowland (L15)

158. Eastoft (L1)

159. Fulbeck (L11)

160. Keelby (L3)

161. Lutton (L14)

162. Old Bolingbroke (L8)

163. Saxby All Saints (L2)

164. Scopwick (L9)

165. Sutterton (L12)

166. Swaby (L7)

167. Swinstead (L13)

168. Tealby (L5)

169. Willoughton(L4)

170. Wragby (L6)
Leicestershire (Lei)

171. Carlton Curlieu (Lei9)

172. Goadby (Lei8)

173. Great Dalby (Lei6)

174. Harby (Lei1)

175. Hathern(Lei2)

176. Markfield (Lei5)

177. Packington (Lei4)

178. Seagrave (Lei3)

179. Sheepy Magna (Lei7)

180. Ullesthorpe(Lei10)
Rutland (R)

181. Empingham (R1))

182. Lyddington (R2)
Northamptonshire (Nth)

183. Kislingbury (Nth4)

184. Little Harrowden (Nth3)

185. Sulgrave (Nth5)

186. Warmington (Nth1)

187. Welford (Nth2)
Huntingdonshire (Hu)

188. Warboys (Hu1)

189. Kimbolton (Hu2)
Cambridgeshire (C)

190. Little Downham (C1)

191. Elsworth (C2)
Norfolk (Nf)

192. Ashwellthorpe(Nf10)

193. Blickling (Nf3)

194. Docking (Nf1)

195. Garboldisham (Nf13)

196. Gooderstone(Nf8)

197. Great Snoring(Nf2)

198. Grimston(NF4)

199. Ludham(Nf6)

200. North Elmham (Nf5)

201. Outwell(Nf7)

202. Pulham St Mary (Nf12)

203. Reedham (Nf11)

204. Shipdham (Nf9)
Suffolk (Sf)

205. Kedington (Sf4)

206. Kersey (Sf5)

207. Mendlesham (Sf2)

208. Tuddenham (Sf1)

209. Yoxford (Sf3)
     Buckinghamshire (Bk)

210. Buckland(Bk4)

211. Coleshill (Bk5)

212. Horton (Bk6)

213. Long Crendon (Bk3)

214. Stewkley (Bk2)

215. Tingewick (Bk1)
     Bedfordshire (Bd)

216. Great Barford (Bd2)

217. Harlington (Bd3)

218. Turvey (Bd1)
     Hertfordshire (Hrt)

219. Codicote (Hrt2)

220. Therfield (Hrt1)

221. Wheathampstead (Hrt3)
     Essex (Ess)

SOUTHERN COUNTIES
Somersetshire (So)

239. Blagdon (So1)

240. Brompton Regis (So9)

241. Coleford(So4)

222. Belchamp Walter (Ess2)

223. Canewdon (Ess15)

224. Cornish Hall End (Ess3)

225. Doddinghurst (Ess14)

226. East Mersea (Ess10)

227. GreatChesterford(Ess1)

228. Henham (Ess4)

229. High Easter (Ess8)

230. Little Baddow (Ess12)

231. Tiptree(Ess9)

232. Tillingham (Ess13)

233. Little Bentley (Ess7)

234. Netteswell (Ess11)

235. Stisted(Ess5)

236. West Bergholt (Ess6)
     Middlesex & London (Mxl)

237. Hackney (MxL2)

238. Harmondsworth (MxL1)

242. Horsington (So11)

243. Merriott (So13)

244. Pitminster (So12)

245. Stogumber (So7)

246. Stogursey (So6)

247. Stoke St Gregory(So10)

248. Wedmore (So3)

249. Weston (So1)

250. Withypool (So8)

251. Wootton Courtenay (So5))
Wiltshire (W)

252. Ashton Keynes (W1)

253. Avebury (W3)

254. Burbage (W4)

255. Fovant (W8)

256. Netheravon (W6)

257. Steeple Ashton (W5)

258. SuttonBenger(W2)

259. Sutton V eny (W7)

260. Whiteparish (W9)
Berkshire (Brk)

261. Buckland (Brk1)

262. Inkpen (Brk4)

263. Swallowfield(Brk5)

264. Uffington (Brk2)

265. West Ilsley (Brk3)
Surrey (Sr)

266. Coldharbour (Sr3)

267. East Clandon (Sr2)

268. Outwood (Sr4)

269. Thursley(Sr5)

270. Walton-on-the-Hill(Sr1)
Kent (K)

271. Appledore (K7)

272. Denton(K5)

273. Farningham (K2)

274. Goudhurst (K6)

275. Staple (K3)

276. Stoke (K1)

277. Warren Street (K4)
Cornwall (Co)

278. Altarnun (Co2)

279. Egloshayle(Co3)

280. Gwinear (Co5)

281. Kilkhampton (Co1)

282. Mullion (Co7)

283. St Buryan (Co6)

284. St Ewe (Co4)
Devonshire (D)

285. Blackawton (D11)

286. Chawleigh (D4)

287. Cornwood (D10)

288. Gittisham(D5)

289. Kennford (D7)

290. Parracombe (D1)

291. Peter Tavy (D8)

292. South Zeal (D6)

293. Swimbridge (D2)

294. Weare Giffard (D3)

295. Widecombe-in-the-Moor (D9)
Dorsetshire (Do)

296. Ansty (Do2)

297. Kingston (Do5)

298. Portesham (Do4)

299. Sixpenny Handley (Do1)

300. Whitchurch Canonicorum (Do3)
Hampshire (Ha)

301. Burley (Ha6)

302. Hambledon(Ha5)

303. Hatherden (Ha1)

304. King's Somborne (Ha3)

305. New Alresford (Ha4)

306. Oakley (Ha2))
Isle of Wight (Ha)

307. Whitwell (Ha7)
Sussex (Sx)

308. East Harting (Sx2)

309. Firle (Sx6)

310. Fletching (Sx4)

311. Horam (Sx5)

312. Sutton (Sx3)

313. Warnham (Sx1)

References

Aceto, Michael. 2004. Eastern Caribbean English–derived language varieties: Phonology. In Bernd Kortmann, Edgar W. Schneider, Kate Burridge, Rajend Mesthrie & Clive Upton (eds.), *A handbook of varieties of English: A multimedia reference tool. Phonology*, 481–499. Berlin: Mouton de Gruyter.

Aceto, Michael. 2010. Dominican Kokoy. In Daniel Schreier, Peter Trudgill, Edgar W. Schneider & Jeffery Williams (eds.), *The lesser–known varieties of English: An introduction*, 171–194. New York: Cambridge University Press.

Alleyne, Mervyn. 1979. On the genesis of language. In Kenneth C. Hill (ed.), *The Genesis of Language*. Ann Arbor: Karoma.

Alleyne, Mervyn. 1980. *Comparative Afro–American*. Ann Arbor: Karoma.

Alleyne, Mervyn. 1996. *Syntaxe historique créole*. Paris: Karthala/Presses Universitaires Créoles.

Amussen, Susan Dwyer. 2009. *Caribbean Exchanges: Slavery and the transformation of English society, 1640–1700*. Sydney, Austrailia: ReadHowYouWant.com.

Arbell, Mordehay. 2002. *The Jewish nation of the Caribbean*. Jerusalem, Israel: Gefen Pub.

Arends, Jacques. 1989. *Syntactic developments in Sranan: Creolization as a gradual process*. Katholieke Universiteit ti Nijmegen dissertation.

Arends, Jacques. 2002. The history of the Surinamese creoles 1: A sociohistorical survey. In Eithne Carlin & Jacques Arends (eds.), *Atlas of the Languages of Suriname*, 115–130. Leiden: KITLV Press.

Arends, Jacques, Pieter Muysken & Norval Smith. 1995. *Pidgins and creoles*. Amsterdam: John Benjamins Publishing Company.

Armitage, David. 2005. The Scottish diaspora. In Jenny Wormald (ed.), *Scotland: A history*, 272–303. Oxford: Oxford University Press.

Atkinson, Q. D. 2011. Phonemic diversity supports a serial founder effect model of language expansion from Africa. *Science* 332(6027). 346–349. DOI:10.1126/science.1199295

Ayearst, Morley. 1960. *The British West Indies: The search for self–government*. New York: New York University Press.

Baissac, Charles. 1880. *Étude sur Le patois créole Mauricien (study on the Mauritian Creole patois)*. Nancy: Imprimerie Berger-Levrault et cie.

References

Baker, Philip. 1998. Investigating the origin and diffusion of shared features among the Atlantic English Creoles. In Philip Baker & Adrienne Bruyn (eds.), *St. Kitts and the Atlantic Creoles: The text of Samuel Augustus Matthews in Perspective*, 315–364. London: University of Westminster Press.

Baker, Philip. 2000. Theories of creolization and the degree and nature of restructuring. In I. Neumann–Holzschuh & Edgar. W. Schneider (eds.), *Degrees of restructuring in creole languages*, 41–64. John Benjamins Publishing Company.

Bannet, Eve Tavor. 2011. *Transatlantic stories and the history of reading, 1720–1810.* Cambridge: Cambridge University Press.

Beal, John. 2004. English dialects in the north of England: Phonology. In Bernd Kortmann, Edgar W. Schneider, Kate Burridge, Rajend Mesthrie & Clive Upton (eds.), *A Handbook of Varieties of English: A Multimedia Reference Tool. Phonology*, 113–34. Berlin: Mouton de Gruyter.

Beckles, Hilary. 1989. *White servitude and black slavery in Barbados, 1627–1715.* Knoxville: Tennessee University Press.

BHO. 2009. *British history online.* http://www.british-history.ac.uk/Default.aspx, accessed 2009-2-12.

Bickerton, Derek. 1975. *Dynamics of A Creole system.* Cambridge: Cambridge University Press.

Bickerton, Derek. 1977. Pidginization and creolization: Language acquisition and language universals. In Albert Valdman (ed.), *Pidgin and creole languages*, 49–69. Bloomington: Indiana University Press.

Bickerton, Derek. 1979. Beginnings. In Kenneth C. Hill (ed.), *The Genesis of Language*, 1–22. Ann Arbor: Karoma.

Bickerton, Derek. 1981/2016. *Roots of language.* Berlin: Language Science Press. DOI:10.17169/langsci.b91.109

Bickerton, Derek. 1984. The language bioprogram hypothesis. *Behavioral and Brain Sciences* 7(02). 173–221. DOI:10.1017/s0140525x00044149

Bickerton, Derek. 1999. How to acquire language without positive evidence: What acquisitionists can learn from creoles. In M DeGraff (ed.), *Language Creation and Language Change: Creolization, Diachrony and Development*, 49–74. Cambridge, Mass: MIT Press.

Blackburn, Robin. 1998. *The making of New World slavery: From the Baroque to the modern, 1492–1800.* London: Verso.

Blake, Renee. 2004. Bajan: Phonology. In Bernd Kortmann, Edgar W. Schneider, Kate Burridge, Rajend Mesthrie & Clive Upton (eds.), *A Handbook of Varieties of English: A Multimedia Reference Tool. Phonology*, 501–508. Berlin: Mouton de Gruyter.

Bloomfield, Leonard. 1933. *Language.* New York: Holt, Rinehart & Winston.

Braun, Maria. 2009. *Word–formation and creolisation: The case of early Sranan* (Linguistische Arbeiten 517). Tübingen: Tübingen.

Brewer, John & Staves Susan. 1996. *Early modern conceptions of property.* London: Routledge.

Bridenbaugh, Carl. 1968. *Vexed and troubled Englishmen, 1590–1642.* Oxford: The Clarendon Press.

Bridenbaugh, Carl & Roberta Bridenbaugh. 1972. *No peace beyond the line: The English in the Caribbean, 1624–1690.* New York: Oxford University Press.

Bruyn, Adrienne. 1995. Relative clauses in early Sranan. In Jacques Arends (ed.), *Relative clauses in early Sranan*, vol. 13 (Creole Language Library), 149–202. Amsterdam: John Benjamins Publishing Company.

Buddingh, Hans. 1995. *Geschiedenis Van Suriname (History of Suriname).* Utrecht: Het Spectrum.

Burg, Barry R. 1995. *Sodomy and the pirate tradition: English sea rovers in the seventeenth century Caribbean.* New York: New York University Press.

Burke, John. 1838. *A genealogical and heraldic history of the commoners of Great Britain and Ireland.* London: H. Colburn.

Bynon, Theodora. 1983. *Historical linguistics.* Cambridge: Cambridge University Press.

Byrne, Francis. 1987. *Grammatical relations in a radical Creole: Verb complementation in Saramaccan.* Amsterdam: John Benjamins Publishing Company.

Campbell, Peter. 1977. Barbados: The early Years. *Journal of Barbados Museum and Historical Society* 35(3). 155–157.

Campbell, Peter. 1984. Aspects of Barbados land tenure, 1627–1663. *Journal of Barbados Museum and Historical Society* 37(2). 112–158.

Campbell, Peter. 1986. *Chapters in Barbados history.* St. Ann's Garrison, Barbados: Barbados Museum & Historical Society.

Campbell, Peter & John Scott. 1993. *Some early Barbadian history.* St. Michael, Barbados: Caribbean Graphics & Letchworth Ltd.

Cassidy, Frederic. 1982. *Jamaica talk: Three Hundred Years of the English language in Jamaica.* Kingston: University of the West Indies Press, (Reprint) 2007.

Cassidy, Frederic & Robert Le Page. 1967. *Dictionary of Jamaican English.* Cambridge & New York: Cambridge University Press.

Chaudenson, Robert. 1979. *Les créoles Français.* Paris: Fernand Nathan.

Chaudenson, Robert. 1992. *Creolization of language and culture.* London: Routledge (Reprint 2001).

Chaudenson, Robert & Salikoko Mufwene. 2001. *Creolization of language and culture.* London: Routledge.

References

Clark, Peter & David Souden. 1988. *Migration and society in Early modern England*. Totowa, N. J.: Barnes & Noble.

Clark, Urszula. 2004. The English West Midlands: Phonology. In Bernd Kortmann, Edgar W. Schneider, Kate Burridge, Rajend Mesthrie & Clive Upton (eds.), *A Handbook of Varieties of English: A Multimedia Reference Tool. Phonology*, 134–163. Berlin: Mouton de Gruyter.

Coldham, Peter. 1987. *The complete Book of Emigrants 1607–1660: A comprehensive listing compiled from English public records of those who took ship to the Americas for political, religious, and Economic reasons; of those who Were deported for vagrancy, roguery, or non–conformity; and of those who Were sold to labour in the new colonies*. Baltimore: Genealogical Pub. Co.

Coldham, Peter. 1988. *The bristol registers of servants sent to foreign plantations, 1654-1686*. Baltimore: Genealogical Pub. Co.

Coldham, Peter. 1992. *The complete Book of Emigrants: 1607–1660*. Baltimore: Genealogical Pub. Co.

Corrigan, Karen P. 2010. *Irish English: Northern Ireland*. Edinburgh: Edinburgh University Press.

Cowles, Michael & Caroline Davis. 1982. On the origins of the .05 level of statistical significance. *American Psychologist* 37(5). 553–558.

Currer–Briggs, Noel. 1982. *Worldwide family history*. London; Boston: Routledge & Kegan Paul.

Davies, Kenneth. 1974. *The North Atlantic world in the seventeenth century*. Minneapolis: University of Minnesota Press.

Davis, Nicholas D. 1887. *The Cavaliers & Roundheads of Barbados, 1650–1652: With some account of the early history of Barbados*. Georgetown: Argosy Press.

DeCamp, David & Ian Hancock (eds.). 1974. *Pidgins and creoles: Current trends and prospects*. Georgetown: Georgetown University Press.

DeCoursey, William. 2003. *Statistics and probability for Engineering applications with Microsoft Excel*. Burlington: Elsevier.

DeGraff, Michel. 2001. *Language creation and language change: Creolization, diachrony, and development*. Cambridge, Mass.: MIT Press.

Denzin, Norman. 1978. *The research act: A theoretical introduction to sociological methods*. New York: McGraw–Hill.

Dobson, David. 2005. *Barbados and Scotland links, 1627–1877*. Baltimore: Clearfield.

Duke, Henning B. 1983. *The house of commons, 1660-1690*. London: Published for the History of Parliament Trust by Secker & Warburg.

Dunn, Richard. 1973. *Sugar and slaves: The rise of the planter class in the English West Indies, 1624–1713*. New York: Norton.

Ehrlich, Avrum M. 2009. *Encyclopedia of the Jewish diaspora: Origins, experiences, and culture.* California: ABC–CLIO.

Elias, Marie L. & Josie Elias. 2010. *Barbados.* New York: Marshall Cavendish Benchmark.

Elliott, John. H. 2007. *Empires of the Atlantic world: Britain and Spain in America 1492–1830.* New Haven: Yale University Press.

Esposito, Barbara, Lee Wood & Kathryn Bardsley. 1982. *Prison slavery.* Washington, D. C.: Committee to Abolish Prison Slavery.

Faber, Eli. 1998. *Jews, Slaves, and the Slave trade: Setting the record straight.* New York: New York University Press.

Ferguson, Charles. 1971. Absence of copula notion of simplicity: A Study of normal speech, baby talk, foreigner talk, and pidgins. In Dell Hymes (ed.), *Pidginization and Creolization of Languages: Proceedings of a Conference Held at the University of the West Indies Mona, Jamaica, April 1968,* 141–150. London: Cambridge University Press.

Fischer, Andreas & Daniel Ammann. 1991. *An index to dialect maps of Great Britain.* Amsterdam: John Benjamins Publishing Company.

Fisher, Frederick, J. Penelope, J. Corfield & Negley B. Harte. 1990. *London and the English economy, 1500–1700.* London: Hambledon Press.

Forsyth, William. 1869. *Cases and opinions on constitutional law: And various points of English jurisprudence, collected and digested from official documents and other sources; with notes.* London: Stevens & Haynes.

Fraser, Henry. 1990. *A–z of Barbadian heritage.* Jamaica: Heinemann Publishers (Caribbean).

Friedman, Saul S. 1999. *Jews and the American Slave trade.* New Brunswick, New Jersey: Transaction Publishers.

Galenson, David W. 2002. *Traders, planters and slaves: Market behavior in early English America.* Cambridge: Cambridge University Press.

Games, Alison. 2008. Migration and Frontiers. In T. Falola & K. D. Roberts (eds.), *The Atlantic World, 1450–2000,* 48–65. Bloomington: Indiana University Press.

Gaunt, Peter. 2003. *The English civil wars, 1642–1651.* Oxford: Osprey.

Godfrey, Sheldon J. & Judy Godfrey. 1995. *Search out the land: The Jews and the growth of equality in British colonial America, 1740–1867.* Montreal; Buffalo: McGill–Queen's University Press.

Goodman, Morris F. 1964. *A comparative study of Creole French dialects* (Series practica 4). Hague: Mouton.

Great Britain House of Lords. 1761. Journals of the House of Lords. In B. Franklin & N. G. Dufief (eds.), *The parliamentary or constitutional history of England: From the earliest times, to the restoration of King Charles II: Collected from the records, the rolls of parliament, the journals of both houses, the public libraries, original manuscripts, scarce speeches, and tracts: All compared with the several contemporary writers, and connected, throughout, with the history of the times*, vol. 12. Printed for J. and R. Tonson and A. Millar, in the Strand, & W. Sandby, in Fleet-Street.

Griffin, Patrick. 2001. *The people with No name: Ireland's Ulster Scots, America's Scots Irish, and the creation of a British Atlantic world, 1689–1764*. Princeton, New Jersey: Princeton University Press.

Griffiths, Ralph & George E Griffiths (eds.). 1797. *The monthly review; or literary journal*. Vol. 24. London: printed for R. Griffiths.

Hall, Robert A. 1953. *Haitian Creole: Grammar, texts, vocabulary* (Memoirs of the American Anthropology Association 74). Philadelphia: American Folklore Society.

Hall, Robert A. 1966. *Pidgin and Creole languages*. Ithaca, New York: Cornell University Press.

Hanks, Reuel. 2011. *Encyclopedia of geography terms, themes, and concepts*. California: ABC-CLIO.

Harlow, Vincent T. 1926. *A history of Barbados, 1625–1685*. Oxford: Clarendon Press.

Healy, Maureen. 1993. The parallel continuum model for Suriname: A preliminary study. In Francis Byrne & John A. Holm (eds.), *Atlantic Meets Pacific: A global view of pidginization and creolization; selected papers from the Society for Pidgin and Creole Linguistics*, vol. 11 (Creole Language Library), 279–289. Amsterdam: John Benjamins Publishing Company.

Henry, Patrick. 1958. A linguistic survey of Ireland. Preliminary report. *Norsk Tidsskrift for Sprogvidenskap* 1. 49–208.

Herlein, J. D. 1718. *Beschrijvinge Van de volk-plantinge Zuriname' – the early Surinamese Creoles in the Suriname Creole archive*. Te Leeuwarden: Meindert Injema.

Heywood, Linda M. & John K. Thornton. 2007. *Central Africans, Atlantic Creoles, and the foundation of the Americas, 1585–1660*. New York: Cambridge University Press.

Hickey, Raymond. 1997. Arguments for creolisation in Irish English. In Raymond Hickey & StanisÓaw Puppel (eds.), *Language history and linguistic modelling. A festschrift for Jacek Fisiak on his 60th birthday*, 969–1038. Berlin: Mouton de Gruyter.

Hickey, Raymond. 2004. *A sound atlas of Irish English*. Berlin; New York: Mouton de Gruyter.

Hinskens, Frans. 2009. The erosion of a variable process. The case of n–deletion in Ripuarian and Limburg dialects of Dutch. In Caroline Féry Frank Kügler & Ruben van de Vijver (eds.), *Variation and gradience in phonetics and phonology*, 311–350. Berlin: Mouton de Gruyter.

Hoefte, Rosemarijn. 1998. *In address of slavery: A social history of British Indian and Javanese laborers in Suriname*. Gainesville: University Press of Florida.

Holm, John. 1988. *Pidgins and Creoles: Theory and structure*. Vol. 1. New York: Cambridge University Press.

Holm, John. 1989. *Pidgins and Creoles: Reference survey*. Vol. 2. New York: Cambridge University Press.

Holm, John. 1994. English in the Caribbean. In Robert Burchfield (ed.), *The Cambridge history of the English language. English in Britain and overseas: Origins and development*, 328–380. Cambridge & New York: Cambridge University Press.

Hornsby, Stephen & Moll Hermann. 2005. *British Atlantic, American frontier: Spaces of power in early modern British America*. Hannover: University Press of New England.

Hotten, John C. 1874. *The original lists of persons of quality: Emigrants; religious Exiles; political rebels; serving men sold for a term of Years; apprentices; children stolen; maidens pressed; and others who went from Great Britain to the American plantations, 1600–1700*. Baltimore: Genealogical Pub. Co.

Huber, Magnus & Mikael Parkvall. 1999. *Spreading the word: The issue of diffusion among the Atlantic Creoles*. London: University of Westminster Press.

Huttar, George L. & Mary L. Huttar. 1994. *Ndyuka*. London: Routledge.

Hymason, Albert M. 1908. *A history of the Jews in England*. London: Chatto & Windus.

Jacobs, Jaap & Hermann Wellenreuther. 2009. *Jacob Leisler's Atlantic world in the later seventeenth century: Essays on religions, militia, trade and networks*. Berlin: Lit. Verlag.

James, Winston. 1998. *Holding aloft the banner of Ethiopia: Caribbean radicalism in Early twentieth–century America*. London: Verso.

Johnson, Emory R. 1922. *History of domestic and foreign commerce of the United States 1*. Washington: Carnegie Institution of Washington.

The Wiltshire Possessions of the Abbess of Shaftesbury. 1862 7.

Kambel, Ellen-Rose & Fergus MacKay. 1999. *The rights of indigenous peoples and Maroons in Suriname*. Copenhagen: International Work Group for Indigenous Affairs.

Kaufman, Will & Heidi S. Macpherson. 2005. *Britain and the Americas: Culture, politics, and history*. California: ABC–CLIO.

Keesing, Roger. 1988. *Melanesian Pidgin and Oceanic substrate.* Stanford: Stanford University Press.

Kennedy, David M., Lizabeth Cohen & Thomas A. Bailey. 2009. *The American pageant.* 14th edn. London: Cengage Learning.

Kenny, Kevin. 2006. *Ireland and the British empire.* Oxford: Oxford University Press.

Kihm, Alain. 1980. *Aspects d'une syntaxe historique: études sur Le créole portugais de guinée-bissau.* Paris: Université de Paris III, Sorbonne nouvelle dissertation.

Kippis, Andrew. 1757. *Biographia Britannica: Or, the lives of the most eminent persons, who have flourished in Great Britain and Ireland, from the earliest ages, down to the present times; collected from the best authorities, both printed and manuscript, and digested in the manner of Mr. Bayle's historical and critical dictionary.* Vol. 4. London: Meadows [u.a.]

Kolb, Eduard. 1979. *Atlas of English sounds.* Bern: Francke.

Kortmann, Bernd & Edgar Schneider. 2004. Introduction: Varieties of English in the British Isles. In Bernd Kortmann, Edgar W. Schneider, Kate Burridge, Rajend Mesthrie & Clive Upton (eds.), *A Handbook of Varieties of English: A Multimedia Reference Tool. Phonology,* 25–35. Berlin: Mouton de Gruyter.

Kramp, Andre. 1983. *Early Creole lexicography: A study of C. L. Schumann's manuscript dictionary of early Sranan.* Leiden: Rijksuniversitet te Leiden dissertation.

Lagart, Bert. 2007. *Tests of Statistical Significance.* http://www.csulb.edu/~msaintg/ppa696/696stsig.htm. http://www.csulb.edu/~msaintg/ppa696/696stsig.htm.

Larget, Bert. 2007. *Probability distribution: R help.* http://www.stat.wisc.edu/~larget/R/prob-R.pdf.

Leads Archive of Vernacular Culture (LAVC). 2009. *Introduction to incidental material documents.* http://www.leeds.ac.uk/library/spcoll/lavc/IMdocs.htm, accessed 2009-7-18.

Lefebvre, Claire. 1998. *Creole genesis and the acquisition of grammar: The case of Haitian Creole* (Cambridge studies in linguistics). Cambridge: Cambridge University Press.

Lefebvre, Claire. 2004. *Issues in the study of Pidgin and Creole languages.* Amsterdam: John Benjamins Publishing Company.

Ligon, Richard. 1673. *A true and exact history of the Island of Barbadoes.* London: Peter Parker.

Lumsden, John S. 1999. Language acquisition and creolization. In M. DeGraff (ed.), *Language Creation and Language Change: Creolization, Diachrony and Development.* Cambridge, Mass.: MIT Press.

Macaulay, Ronald K. S. 1977. Review of the linguistic atlas of Scotland: Scots section. *Language Journal of the Linguistic Society of America* 53(1). 224–228.

MacMillan, William M. 1970. *The road to self–rule: A study in colonial evolution.* Freeport, New York: Books for Libraries Press.

Manning, Roger B. 2006. *An apprenticeship in arms: The origins of the British army 1585–1702.* Oxford & New York: Oxford University Press.

Marley, David. 2005. *Historic cities of the Americas: An illustrated encyclopedia.* California: ABC–CLIO.

Mather, James Y. & H. H Speitel (eds.). 1975. *The linguistic atlas of Scotland: Scots section 1.* Hamden, Conn.: Archon Books.

McCusker, John J. & Russell R. Menard. 1991. *The economy of British America, 1607–1789.* 2nd edn. Chapel Hill: University of North Carolina Press.

McWhorter, John H. 1998. Identifying the Creole prototype: Vindicating a typological class. *Language* 74(4). 788–818.

McWhorter, John H. 2000. *Language change and language contact in Pidgins and Creoles.* Amsterdam & Philadelphia: John Benjamins Publishing Company.

McWhorter, John H. 2005. *Defining Creole.* New York: Oxford University Press.

McWhorter, John H. 2011. *Linguistic simplicity and complexity: Why do languages undress?* Berlin: de Gruyter.

Menard, Russell R. 2006. *Sweet negotiations: Sugar, slavery, and plantation agriculture in early Barbados.* Charlottesville: University of Virginia Press.

Mogge, Willem. 1677. *Caerte ofte vertooninge Vande rivieren Van Suriname En commenwijne met verscheyde creken uyt deselue spruijtende als para surinoo En cotteca Ende ander meergelyck die nu tegen woordich bewoont verden [map of the Surinam and Commewijne rivers. Cartographic elements include scale, compass rose, location of rivers, settlements, and fort].* Amsterdam.

Morgan, Kenneth. 1993. *Bristol and the Atlantic trade in the eighteenth century.* Cambridge: Cambridge University Press.

Morgan, Phillip. 2011. *The Cambridge world history of slavery: A. D. 1420–A. D. 1804.* Eltis David, Stanley L. Engerman, K. Bradley & Paul Cartledge (eds.). Vol. 3. Cambridge: Cambridge University Press.

Mufwene, Salikoko. 1990. Pidgins and Creoles. *World Englishes* 9. 98–103.

Mufwene, Salikoko. 1996a. Creole genesis: A population genetic perspective. In Mervyn C. Alleyne & Pauline Christie (eds.), *Caribbean Language Issues, Old & New: Papers in Honour of Professor Mervyn Alleyne on the Occasion of His Sixtieth Birthday,* 163–196. Barbados: University of the West Indies Press.

Mufwene, Salikoko. 1996b. The founder principle in Creole genesis. *Diachronica* 13(1). 83–134.

References

Mufwene, Salikoko. 2001. *The ecology of language evolution: Cambridge approaches to language contact.* Cambridge & New York: Cambridge University Press.

Mufwene, Salikoko. 2008a. *Language evolution: Contact, competition and change.* London: Continuum.

Mufwene, Salikoko. 2008b. What do creoles and pidgins tell us about the evolution of language? In Bernard Laks (ed.), *Origin and evolution of languages: Approaches, models, paradigms,* 272–297. Equinox.

Muysken, Pieter & Norval Smith. 1986. Substrata versus universals in creole genesis: Papers from the Amsterdam creole workshop, April 1985. In *Creole Language Library,* 1–14. John Benjamins Publishing Company.

Nicholas, Thomas. 1872. *Annals and antiquities of the counties and county families of Wales: Containing a record of all ranks of the gentry ... With many ancient pedigrees and memorials of old and extinct families.* London: Longmans, Green, Reader.

Orton, Harold & Michael V. Barry. 1970. *Survey of English dialects: The West midland counties.* Vol. 2. Leeds: E. J. Arnold & Son.

Orton, Harold & Eugen Dieth. 1962. *Survey of English dialects.* Vol. 1. Leeds: E. J. Arnold & Son.

Orton, Harold, W. J. Halliday & M. V. Barry. 1962–71. *Survey of English dialects: Basic materials. Introduction and 4 vols. (each in 3 parts).* Leeds: E. J. Arnold & Son.

Orton, Harold & Philip M. Tilling. 1970. *Survey of English dialects: The East midland counties and East Anglia. Vol. 2.* Leeds: E. J. Arnold & Son.

Page, Eimer. 1997. *Postcolonial discourse in wide sargasso sea.* http://www.qub.ac.uk/imperial/carib/sargasso.htm, accessed 1997-5-13.

Paravisini–Gebert, Lizabet. 1996. *Phyllis Shand Allfrey: A Caribbean life.* New Brunswick, New Jersey: Rutgers University Press.

Parker, Matthew. 2011. *The sugar barons: Family, corruption, empire and War.* London: Hutchinson.

Parry, David. 1977. *The survey of Anglo-Welsh dialects. 1. The South-East.* Swansea: University College.

Parry, David. 1979. *The survey of Anglo-Welsh dialects. 2. The South-West.* Swansea: University College.

Penhallurick, Robert. 1991. *The Anglo–Welsh dialects of North Wales: A survey of conservative rural spoken English in the counties of Gwynedd and Clwyd.* Frankfurt am Main: Peter Lang.

Penhallurick, Robert. 2004. Welsh English: Phonology. In Bernd Kortmann, Edgar W. Schneider, Kate Burridge, Rajend Mesthrie & Clive Upton (eds.), *A handbook of varieties of English: A multimedia reference tool. Phonology*, 98–113. Berlin: Mouton de Gruyter.

Pepys, Samuel & Richard G. Braybrooke. 1848. *Diary and correspondence of Samuel Pepys, m. A. F. R. S.: Secretary to the admiralty in the reigns of Charles II. And James II. With a life and notes.* London: H. Colburn.

Perl, Matthais. 1995. Part II: Saramaccan. In Jacques Arends & Matthias Perl (eds.), *Early Suriname Creole texts: A collection of 18th century Sranan and Saramaccan documents.* Frankfurt-am-Main: Vervuert.

Plag, Ingo & Christian Uffmann. 2000. Phonological restructuring in Creole: The development of paragoge in Sranan. In I Neumann–Holzschuh & Edgar. W. Schneider (eds.), *Degrees of restructuring in Creole languages* (Creole Language Library 22), 243–50. Amsterdam: John Benjamins Publishing Company.

Powell, John. 2005. *Encyclopedia of North American immigration.* New York: Facts On File.

Pugh, Ralph B. & Elizabeth Crittall. 1957. *Parliamentary history: 1629-1660.* http://www.britishhistory.ac.uk/report.aspx?compid=116090.

R Core Team. 2011. *An Introduction to R.* http://cran.r-project.org/doc/manuals/R-intro.html#Top (). http://cran.r-project.org/doc/manuals/R-intro.html#Top.

Redfield, Peter. 2000. *Space in the tropics: From convicts to rockets in French Guiana.* Berkeley: University of California Press.

Rens, Lucien L. E. 1953. *The historical and social background of Surinam's Negro-English.* Amsterdam: North-Holland Pub. Co. Reprint, Hong Kong: forgottenbooks.org, 2010.

RHS. 1924. *Camden miscellany.* Vol. 13. Great Britain: Royal Historical Society.

Roca, Iggy & Wyn Johnson. 1999. *A course in phonology.* Oxford: Blackwell Publishers.

Rogers, James E. T. 1889. *The economic interpretation of history: Lecturers delivered in Worcester college hall, Oxford, 1887–1888.* London: G. P. Putnam's Sons.

Roper, Louis H. & Bertrand Van Ruymbeke. 2007. *Constructing early modern empires: Proprietary ventures in the Atlantic world, 1500–1750.* Leiden: Brill.

Sacks, David H. 1993. *Bristol and the Atlantic economy, 1450–1700.* Berkeley: University of California Press.

Sainsbury, Noel (ed.). 1860. *America and West Indies: February 1652.* London. http://www.britishhistory.ac.uk/report.aspx?compid=69255&strquery=150, %201860, accessed 2011-10-17.

References

Sainsbury, Noel (ed.). 1880. *America and West Indies: May 1668*. London. http://www.britishhistory.ac.uk/report.aspx?compid=76523&strquery=67+persons, %201880, accessed 2011-10-13.

Sainsbury, Noel (ed.). 1889. *America and West Indies: January 1672*. London. http://www.britishhistory.%20ac.uk/report.aspx?compid=70219&strquery=1671, %201889, accessed 2009-12-10.

Sainsbury, Noel (ed.). 1893. *America and West Indies: January 1675*. London. http://www.britishhistory.ac.uk/report.aspx?compid=70090, accessed 2009-12-8.

Sainsbury, Noel & John W. Fortescue (eds.). 1889. *America and West Indies: February 1680*. London. http://www.british-history.ac.uk/report.aspx?compid=69999&strquery=%20surinam%201889, accessed 2011-10-16.

Salomon, Frank & Stuart B. Schwartz. 1999. *Cambridge history of the native peoples of the Americas*. Vol. 3, South America, Part 2. Cambridge: Cambridge University Press.

Saxon, Lyle. 1989. *Fabulous New Orleans*. Louisiana: Pelican Publishing.

Schaefer, Christina. K. 1998. *Genealogical encyclopedia of the colonial Americas: A complete digest of the records of all the countries of the Western hemisphere*. Baltimore: Genealogical Pub. Co.

Schumann, C. L. 1783. *Neger–Englisches wörterbuch*. http://www.sil.org/americas/suriname/Schumann/National/SchumannGerDict.html, accessed 2007-10-12.

Siegel, Jeff. 1985. Koines and koineization. *Language in Society* 14(3). 357–378.

Siegel, Jeff. 2004. Koine formation and Creole genesis. In Norval Smith & Tonjes Veenstra (eds.), *Creole language library*, 175–198. Amsterdam & Philadelphia: John Benjamins Publishing Company.

Smith, Abbot E. & IEAHC. 1947. *Colonists in bondage: White servitude and convict labor in America, 1607–1776*. Williamsburg: Institute of Early American History, Culture & University of North Carolina Press.

Smith, Norval. 1977. Vowel epithesis in the Surinam Creoles. *Amsterdam Studies* 1. 1–31.

Smith, Norval. 1987. *The genesis of the Creole languages of Surinam*. Amsterdam: Universiteit van Amsterdam dissertation.

Smith, Norval. 2002. The Creole languages of Surinam: Past and present. In Eithne Carlin & Jacques Arends (eds.), *Atlas of the languages of Suriname*, 131–151. Leiden: KITLV Press.

Smith, Norval. 2006. Very rapid creolization in the restricted motivation hypothesis. In Claire Lefebvre, Lydia White & Christine Jourdan (eds.), *L2 acquisition and Creole genesis: Dialogues*, 49–65. Amsterdam: John Benjamins Publishing Company.

Smith, Norval. 2008a. Creole phonology. In Silvia Kouwenberg & John V. Singler (eds.), *Handbook of Pidgin and Creole studies.* Chichester; Malden, MA: Wiley-Blackwell Pub. DOI:10.1002/9781444305982.ch5

Smith, Norval. 2008b. The origin of the Portuguese words in Saramaccan: Implications for sociohistory. In Susanne Michaelis (ed.), *Roots of creole structures: Weighing the contribution of substrates and superstrates,* 153–168. Amsterdam: John Benjamins Publishing Company.

Smith, Norval. 2009. English–Speaking in Surinam? In Jacques. Arends, Rachel. Selbach, Hugo. C. Cardoso & Margot van den Berg (eds.), *Gradual Creolization: Studies Celebrating Jacques Arends,* vol. 34 (Creole Language Library), 305–326. Amsterdam & Philadelphia: John Benjamins Publishing Company.

Smith, Norval & Vinije Haabo. 2004. Suriname Creoles: Phonology. In Bernd Kortmann, Edgar W. Schneider, Kate Burridge, Rajend Mesthrie & Clive Upton (eds.), *A handbook of varieties of English: A multimedia reference tool. Phonology,* 525–566. Berlin: Mouton de Gruyter.

Smith, Norval & Tonjes Veenstra. 2001. *Creolization and contact.* Amsterdam: John Benjamins Publishing Company.

Stevenson, A. (ed.). 1823. *John Holtrop's English and Dutch dictionary.* Dordrecht: Blussé en van Braam.

Stichting, Volkslectuur. 1980. *Woordenlijst Sranan–Nederlands–English: Met een lijst van planten– en dierennamen.* Paramaribo: Vaco.

Thomas, Collins R. & Joseph S. Wood. 1999. *One life at a time: A new world family narrative, 1630–1960.* Oakton, Va: Ravensyard Pub.

Trudgill, Peter. 2002. The history of the lesser–known varieties of English. In Richard Watts & Peter Trudgill (eds.), *Alternative histories of English,* 29–44. London: Routledge.

Trudgill, Peter. 2004. The dialect of East Anglia: Phonology. In Bernd Kortmann, Edgar. W. Schneider, Kate Burridge, Rajend Mesthrie & Clive Upton (eds.), *A handbook of varieties of English: A multimedia reference tool. Phonology,* 167–177. Berlin: Mouton de Gruyter.

Tuten, Donald N. 2003. *Koineization in medieval Spanish.* Berlin: Mouton de Gruyter.

VCDH. 2009. *Address of origin names in Bristol registers (1654–1686).* http://www.virtualjamestown.org/indentures/advsearch_bristol.html, accessed 2009-7-11.

VCDHb. 2009. *Virtual Jamestown registers of servants sent to foreign plantations.* http://www.virtualjamestown.org/indentures/about_indentures.html, accessed 2009-7-11.

Viereck, Wolfgang. 1990. *The computer–developed linguistic atlas of England.* Tübingen: Niemeyer.

Viereck, Wolfgang. 1997. The computer developed linguistic atlas of England, volume 1 (1991) and 2 (1997): Dialectological, computational and interpretative aspects. *ICAME Journal* 21. 79–90.

Vieyra, Anthony. 1860. *A dictionary of the English and Portuguese languages: In two parts,English and Portuguese, and Portuguese and English.* Lisbon: Printed for F. Wingrave.

Von Fermin, Philippe. 1769. *Description générale, historique, géographie et physique de La colonie de Surinam.* Amsterdam: E. van Harrevelt.

Ward, Martha. 2004. *Voodoo Queen: The spirited lives of Marie Laveau.* Jackson: University Press of Mississippi.

Watts, David. 1990. *The West Indies: Patterns of development, culture and environmental change since 1492.* Cambridge: Cambridge University Press.

Wells, John C. 1982. *Accents of English.* Vol. 2. Cambridge: Cambridge University Press.

Wheeler, James S. 2002. *The Irish and British wars, 1637–1654: Triumph, tragedy, and failure.* London: Routledge.

Whitehead, Neil. 1996. Northeastern South America (c. 1500–1900). In Bruce G. Trigger, Wilcomb E. Washburn, Richard E. W. Adams, Frank Salomon, Murdo. J. Macleod & Stuart. B. Schwartz (eds.), *The Cambridge history of the native peoples of the Americas,* 382–442. Cambridge: Cambridge University Press.

Williams, Jeffrey. 2003. The establishment and perpetuation of anglophone white enclave communities in the Eastern Caribbean: The case of Island Harbor, Anguilla. In Michael Aceto & Jeffery Williams (eds.), *Contact Englishes of the Eastern Caribbean,* 95–119. Amsterdam: John Benjamins Publishing Company.

Wilner, John. 1992. *Wortubuku ini Sranan Tongo (Sranan Tongo – English dictionary).* 2nd edn. Paramaribo, Suriname: Summer Institute of Linguistics.

Wilner, John. 2003. *Wortubuku ini Sranan Tongo (Sranan Tongo – English dictionary).* 4th edn. Summer Institute of Linguistics.

Wilner, John. 2007. *Wortubuku ini Sranan Tongo (Sranan Tongo – English dictionary).* 5th edn. Paramaribo, Suriname: Summer Institute of Linguistics.

Wroughton, John. 2006. *The Routledge companion to the Stuart age, 1603–1714.* London; New York: Routledge.

Wurm, Stephen, Peter Mühlhäusler & Darrell Tryon. 1996. *Atlas of languages of intercultural communication in the Pacific, Asia and the Americas.* Berlin; New York: Mouton de Gruyter.

Young, Peter & Michael Roffe. 1973. *The English Civil War armies.* Oxford: Osprey Publishing.

Zahedieh, Nuala. 2001. Overseas expansion and trade. In William R. Louis, Nicholas P. Canny & Alaine Low (eds.), *The origins of empire: British overseas enterprise to the close of the seventeenth century*, 398–422. Oxford: Oxford University Press.

Name index

Language index

Subject index

www.ingramcontent.com/pod-product-compliance
Lightning Source LLC
Chambersburg PA
CBHW080914100426
42812CB00007B/2266